SUTTON PUBLISHING

First published in 2002 by
Sutton Publishing Limited · Phoenix Mill
Thrupp · Stroud · Gloucestershire · GL5 2BU

Reprinted in 2002

British Library Cataloguing in Publication Data
A catalogue record for this book is available from the British Library

ISBN 0 7509 2610 4

For Sam

Typeset in 11/12 pt Ehrhardt.
Typesetting and origination by
Sutton Publishing Limited.
Printed and bound in England by
J.H. Haynes & Co. Ltd, Sparkford.

Contents

Acknowledgements

I am grateful to everyone who shared their Home Guard memories with me, and whose personal recollections form such a vital part of this book.

Frank and Joan Shaw have been extremely generous in allowing me to draw without hindrance from their splendid volume *We Remember the Home Guard*. I am also indebted to the individual contributors to that book who have permitted me to quote from their respective accounts. Chris Blount of BBC Radio Cornwall has given me access to his 1991 oral documentary on the subject from which I have drawn on Rex Davey's memories and Eric Higgs's account of the events surrounding 7 September 1940. Bill Griffin, of the Choughs Association at Newquay, supplied me with a great deal of information and literature relating to the Home Guard in his part of the world, including Captain W.A. Owen's vivid eye-witness account of the London Stand Down parade (contained in the Choughs Annual Register of 1944). I am indebted to the many – and mainly unknown – authors of various Home Guard Battalion histories, a large number of which were printed and circulated privately. They all proved invaluable to me in my research. My chapter about Britain's 'Secret Army' would not have been possible without the help of David Lampe's definitive account of the subject, *The Last Ditch*, from which source much of the background information was drawn. Equally vital was the personal memoir written by Frederick J. Simpson of Dorset, which describes in detail his experiences as a member of Auxiliary Units. I am most grateful to him for allowing me to quote from it at such length. *Bombers & Mash: The Domestic Front 1939–1945* by Raynes Minns yielded valuable background information for my chapter about women in the Home Guard.

I should like to thank the following for the use of copyright material:

The Phoney War (Michael Joseph, London, 1961), E.S. Turner and reproduced by permission of Penguin Books Ltd.; *The Last Ditch* (1968), David Lampe and Cassell plc; *From Dusk Till Dawn* (1945), A.G. Street, Cassell plc and Blandford Press; *Please You Draw Near* (1969), Ernest Raymond and Cassell plc; *The Collected Essays, Journalism and Letters of George Orwell*, Volume Two: *My Country Right or Left* (1968), A.M. Heath & Co. Ltd. on behalf of Bill Hamilton as the Literary Executor of the Estate of the late Sonia Brownell Orwell and Martin Secker & Warburg Ltd.; *The Home Guard of Britain* by Charles Graves (Hutchinson 1943), reprinted by permission of the Random House Group Ltd.; *The Real Dad's Army* by Norman Longmate (Hutchinson 1974), David Bolt

Associates; four lines from 'Watching Post' from the *Complete Poems of C. Day Lewis* (Sinclair-Stevenson 1992), the Estate of C. Day Lewis; *Civilians at War: Journals 1938–1946* (1984), George Beardmore and John Murray (Publishers) Ltd.; *Hare Joins the Home Guard* (Wm. Collins 1941), the Trustees of the Alison Uttley Literary Property Trust; *Memoirs of the Forties* by Julian Maclaren-Ross (Sphere Books Ltd. edn., MacDonald & Co. 1991), the late Alan Ross; *Further Particulars* (1987), C.H. Rolph, Oxford University Press and David Higham Associates; extracts from messages and broadcasts by King George VI, the Registrar of the Royal Archives; various letters, documents and publications issued by the War Office, extracts from Sir Edward Grigg's speech to the House of Commons and Sir Winston Churchill's third anniversary message to the Home Guard, the Controller of Her Majesty's Stationery Office. The originals of the documents from which many of the contemporary extracts in this book are taken are held in the Public Record Office. I have made every effort to contact all copyright holders. Any omissions are entirely unintentional, and I would be pleased to rectify them (upon notification) in any subsequent edition of this work. Lastly, my greatest thanks go to Jonathan Falconer at Sutton Publishing for guiding me through this project, Bernadette Walsh for her support and Bill Pertwee for generously contributing a Foreword.

Picture Credits

I am grateful to the following for the supply and use of photographic material:

The Trustees of the Imperial War Museum, London; W.J. Amesbury, Stewart Angell, Tom Bray, Frank Bryant, Lewis Creed, Harry Edwards, Graham Emery, Richard Ewing, Adrian Hoare, Edward Horne, Pamela Housden, June Iddon, Henry Jones, Peggy McGeoch, Rae MacGregor, Raymond Porter, Freda Robjohns, G.B. Rogers (for his original cartoon), Frederick J. Simpson, Major P.J.R. Waller, Melville Watts, Phyllis Woodham, R.P. Wooler.

Foreword

Memories of the actual Local Defence Volunteers, later the Home Guard, came flooding back to me during the day of the first rehearsal of television's *Dad's Army* (and my role as Chief Air Raid Warden Hodges).

In June 1940, my mother and I were staying with my aunt and uncle at Belvedere in Kent. On the night of Anthony Eden's broadcast asking for volunteers to help fight a possible German invasion force, my uncle went straight down to the local police station to enlist. Uncle Bill Tobin was a strapping great Irishman of 6 ft 3 in who had been through the First World War; in fact he was a boy bugler in the Boer War. In one encounter with the Germans during the First World War he had single-handedly silenced an enemy machine-gun crew by, believe it or not, strangling them! So you can see he was slightly eccentric and pretty courageous. Just the sort of man Anthony Eden hoped would answer his call. On the night in question Uncle Bill said to the police sergeant on duty at the station, 'I'm Captain Tobin (his rank in the First World War) and I'm taking command of the local volunteers'. Apparently, so we heard afterwards, the police sergeant hadn't listened to Eden's broadcast and thought that here was some lunatic playing games. He proceeded to try and calm my uncle. Rather like the great radio comedian of the day, Robb Wilton, he started shuffling some papers about on his desk and

Bill Pertwee.

licking his pencil. My uncle told him he'd be back when he had pulled himself together. He then went home and, using his obvious strength, started taking the large furniture – table, chairs, sideboard, bookcases, etc. – out of the house and laying it across the road like a barricade. My aunt, who was Brazilian like my mother, just laughed at anything her husband did, and filling up the road with her furniture was just another one of his eccentric acts. My uncle's final remark on the matter seemed even more eccentric. 'Well, they won't get through tonight.' You can imagine my astonishment when I first read Jimmy Perry and David Croft's script for the Columbia feature film of *Dad's Army* that we did in the early 1970s. Here was Captain Mainwaring assembling a roadblock of household furniture at Walmington-on-Sea. When I told the writers about my uncle's antics they too were astonished, as they had seriously thought of cutting out the furniture scene from the script because it seemed just too ridiculous. Fact certainly is stranger than fiction as they say.

This was only one of the incidents I remember from those strange days of 1940. Soon after the episode concerning my uncle, my mother and I moved into a bungalow on Dartford Heath, also in Kent. There, we were not only a mile or so from a huge gathering of anti-aircraft guns based on the heath but we were also directly under, or so it seemed, the majority of air battles being fought out in the summer skies between the fighters and bombers of the Luftwaffe and our own Spitfires and Hurricanes. During these battles there were several instances that concerned the Home Guard. I remember a Heinkel bomber coming over very low one afternoon as I was walking up the road from the bus-stop after my college studies. The plane seemed to be dropping all sorts of things on to the surrounding area to lighten its load on its way back to Germany. In fact, it was so low I could see the front gunner in his turret. I dived into a ditch soiling my blazer in the process. When I got home I told my mother what had happened. 'Oh, don't worry,' she said. 'Mr Stewart next door is in the Home Guard. He'll sort it out.' That remark typified what nearly everyone thought about the Home Guard. They were the guardians of the civilian population, and this feeling had developed very quickly. The Home Guard, of course, were among us all every day of the week because most of them worked in jobs and services that were a part of our everyday lives.

One morning, on looking into the field adjoining our bungalow, a German airman could be seen floating to earth on his parachute. He was neatly folding his 'chute when suddenly two Home Guardsmen cycling along the road threw down their bikes, scrambled through the hedge and, waving some sort of implement, started dancing round him while shouting and using threatening gestures. I saw the German take off his sleeveless flying jacket and hand it to one of the Guards, displaying his full pilot's tunic, while the Home Guardsmen continued dancing around him. I went out into the garden just as a policeman arrived on the scene. He took out his notebook and quite obviously asked the Guards for their names. Then he ushered them to one side and started talking to the pilot, who kept silent and looked completely bewildered. The policeman and Home Guardsmen then marched him off towards the main gate of the field, with the policeman still writing in his notebook. My immature imagination began to wonder if the policeman was asking him where he came from and what was he doing in the field at 11.02 on a Saturday morning? Well, I thought, Robb Wilton would have asked those kinds of questions in his radio comedy monologues. My mother had apparently been watching this event from the bungalow. When I got in she said, 'You shouldn't interfere. It's nothing to do with you and, anyway, he's some mother's son.' A strange observation in wartime but I suppose she was right. (The saying very much came back to us in 1941 when my brother was killed in the Air Force.)

There is absolutely no doubt at all that if the Germans had invaded our island the Home Guard would have given their lives in what would have been a courageous and brave struggle against huge odds which it would have been nigh-on impossible to overcome. They were the guardians of the people and proud of the duty they had been asked to fulfil. The Captain Mainwarings and Corporal Joneses were in evidence in almost every Home Guard platoon in the country. The Sergeant Wilsons would probably have treated matters slightly more casually, and perhaps used that well-known phrase of his when annoyed with someone, 'Why don't you just clear off?'

This book really tells it all in great detail, and David Carroll certainly deserves a pat on the back for reminding us of that momentous period in our history, and for recalling those who were prepared to give everything of themselves in order to protect their civilian brothers and sisters who slept more peacefully in their beds because of the presence of the Home Guard.

CHAPTER 1

Alexander's Rag-Time Army?

There is an affecting little song which has proved to be extremely popular in recent years and whose laconic opening line proclaims that '. . . it started with a kiss'. Well, needless to say, the Home Guard did not begin in that way at all, although its origins were arguably almost as spontaneous; barely more than a brief flurry of hastily-convened meetings held at the War Office during that warm, unique and – for anyone who lived through it – never to be forgotten spring of 1940. It was a time, of course, when Britain lay vulnerable, seemingly defenceless and dauntingly ripe for the taking by Hitler's massive War Machine. By this time, after all, the German army had already occupied Austria and Czechoslovakia; Poland, Holland and Belgium had suffered the same fate and, with the imminent surrender of France, the narrow English Channel would be all that separated Britain from the unthinkable prospect of Nazi domination.

The Ministry of Information, in co-operation with the War Office, issued a leaflet entitled 'If the Invader Comes . . .', which listed a series of rules for the civilian population at home to follow should they wake up one morning to find the enemy at their door.

1. If the Germans come by parachute, aeroplane or ship, you must remain where you are.
2. Do not believe rumours and do not spread them.
3. Keep watch. If you see anything suspicious, note it carefully and go at once to the nearest police officer or station.
4. Do not give the German anything.
   Do not tell him anything.
   Hide your food and your bicycles.
   Hide your maps.
   See that the enemy gets no petrol.
5. Think before you act. BUT THINK ALWAYS OF YOUR COUNTRY BEFORE YOU THINK OF YOURSELF.

No one who read these stark instructions could fail to realise the gravity of Britain's position. C.H. Rolph, who was (among other things) a journalist and broadcaster, recalled 'that desperate document, which should have been so frightening but which no one remembers', in his memoirs *Further Particulars*. 'It may be that I remember it because I saw some parcels of these messages of

Issued by the Ministry of Information in co-operation with the War Office and the Ministry of Home Security.

If the
INVADER
comes

WHAT TO DO — AND HOW TO DO IT

This was one of a number of leaflets issued on the same theme during the early days of the war. Over fourteen million copies were printed and delivered to households throughout Britain. It has been suggested that the art historian Kenneth (later Lord) Clark and author and diplomat Sir Harold Nicolson were its authors. (HMSO)

controlled panic stacked in our City ARP office – the leaflets were to be delivered by hand, not by post. The bundles had been piled, temporarily and untidily, in an ill-chosen corner near a much-used door, and someone accidentally sent them spinning across the floor. Two parcels burst open, and anyone with a fanciful mind could have seen it as an omen.'

On the evening of 14 May, in the light of the ever-worsening situation at home, and with the widespread fear that an invasion was possible almost by the hour, the newly-appointed War Minister Anthony Eden made a BBC broadcast that was to have an enormous impact on many of those people listening. It would also lead very swiftly to the creation of the largest civilian army that this country had ever gathered together. It is not hard to picture the scene – in that pre-television age – as families throughout the land huddled around their wireless sets to hear what the speech contained. Holland had surrendered on that same day, France would follow suit a month later and the Dunkirk evacuation was imminent. These were truly some of Britain's darkest hours and, at 9.10 p.m., after the routine news bulletin had been read by the BBC announcer Frank Phillips, the microphone was handed over to Mr Eden, whose voice came over the air-waves, piercing the metaphorical gloom.

In view of the grave national situation, listeners must have wondered what on earth was coming but, quite unknown to the general public, the Under-Secretary of State at the Home Office had sent earlier in the day two telegrams to Chief Constables throughout the country preparing the police force for the War Minister's announcement. 'Since the war began,' Eden explained, 'the Government have received countless enquiries from all over the kingdom from men of all ages, who are for one reason or another not at present engaged in military service and who wish to do something for the defence of their country. Well, here is your opportunity. We want large numbers of such men in Great Britain, who are British subjects, between the ages of seventeen and sixty-five, to come forward now and offer their services. . . . The name of the new force which is now to be raised will be the Local Defence Volunteers. This name describes its duties in three words. . . . You will not be paid but you will receive a uniform and you will be armed. . . . In order to volunteer, what you have to do is to give in your name at your local police station; and then, as and when we want you, we will let you know. . . . Here, then, is the opportunity for which so many of you have been waiting. Your loyal help, added to the arrangements which already exist, will make and keep our country safe.'

Whitehall issued a statement on the subject simultaneously with Eden's broadcast. Volunteers should be '. . . men of reasonable physical fitness and with a knowledge of firearms', it read. 'The need is greatest in small towns, villages and less densely populated areas. The duties of the force can be undertaken in a volunteer's spare time. . . .'

Of course, civilian armies of this kind were by no means a new concept. Indeed, they had a distinguished pedigree, as Major E.A. Mackay in his *History of the Wiltshire Home Guard* (1946) so eloquently pointed out. 'The trained bands of Elizabeth; the Somerset men raised against Monmouth; the Fencibles of the North; the Militia and Yeomanry and the Loyal Corps of Infantry of the South, raised to repel the invasion of Bonaparte; the National Reserve of the last Great War, and now the Home Guard. Truly a wonderful cavalcade. Stout hearts determined to defend their beloved [country] to their last breath. . . .'

Although Eden's speech undoubtedly came as a great surprise to nearly everyone who heard it on the evening of 14 May, there had nevertheless been a growing desire among people up and down the country who were not directly engaged in the war for the opportunity to provide some form of localised defence in the event of an invasion. This impulse manifested itself in a variety of ways, but is perhaps best illustrated in the highly organised and colourful example of the well documented Much Marcle Watchers, whose existence was recorded by Charles Graves in *The Home Guard of Britain* (1943): 'It was a bright spring afternoon of March 1940 that a lady had called at the Battalion Headquarters of the KSLI stationed at Ross-on-Wye. She . . . said she was

Men of all ages queuing up to sign on as Local Defence Volunteers in the wake of War Minister Eden's appeal. (IWM)

alarmed at the possibility of German parachute troops landing in the thinly populated areas of Herefordshire and the Welsh Border. She had therefore organised her staff and tenantry, to the number of eighty, into bands of watchers, whom she had stationed on the high ground in the vicinity of the ancestral home at Much Marcle. These men went on duty each night and everyone had a white arm-band stencilled "Much Marcle Watchers". She asked for the loan of eighty rifles and some ammunition, "with a couple of machine guns if you have any."' Needless to say, the Battalion Commander turned down her request, but there is no doubt that she embodied the spirit of the times. 'There, two months before the LDV were born,' commented Graves, 'was the first Home Guard complete with watchers, brassards, organisation, even to lack of arms.'

The response to Eden's broadcast was both immediate and overwhelming, and queues began forming at police stations almost before the War Minister had finished speaking. Bertram Miller of Ilford, Essex, who had been a sergeant in the Royal Engineers during the First World War, was among the earliest volunteers to enrol. 'At the end of the appeal I rose from my chair and reached for my jacket that was hanging behind the door. . . . I made my way to Ilford Police Station, thinking I might be the first person to offer his services in my locality, but on arrival I found that I had just been beaten by a Mr Jack Louis.

An LDV Recruiting Rally at Poole, Dorset. (IWM)

The police were surprised as they had not received any official instructions. However, they got busy on the telephone and eventually took our names and addresses. Shortly afterwards we received a letter asking us to report to a temporary headquarters in Cranbrook Road, Ilford, where we met our new Commanding Officer. . . . We were split into groups or sections of twelve who were living fairly close together. . .'.

Ron Yates listened to the broadcast at home in Preston. 'I went along to Earl Street Central Police Station that same evening after convincing my mother that it was my duty, especially as I was in a reserved occupation on skilled war work. I must have been the eighty-sixth volunteer there that evening in Preston, for that was the number with which I was issued.'

In Monmouthshire, too, as Captain Warren Jenkins explained in his history of the 6th Battalion Monmouthshire Home Guard, the response '. . . was truly staggering. The police stations, drill halls and, at Rhymney, the Brewery Offices, that had been temporarily converted into Recruiting Stations for the new army, were beseiged. During that night and throughout the succeeding days and nights harassed police officials, backed by volunteers, strove valiantly to enrol, tabulate and, as far as was humanly possible, advise members as to future action.

Overnight an army was born, a people's army, a child of the people. No shrinking infant, but a vigorous and decidedly healthy child. . . .'

The obvious sense of relief that many men felt now that there was something tangible they could do to help fend off a possible invasion, was captured by George Beardmore in his wartime diary (published in 1984 under the title *Civilians at War*). He lived in Harrow and worked as a clerk at Broadcasting House in the heart of London. 'Dreadful, unthinkable visions enter my head of what would happen if [Germany] won and crossed the Channel. Mentally I have already sent [my wife and baby daughter] to Canada, and seen Harrow bombed, and parachutists seize Broadcasting House. The imagination makes these fantastic notions so real, but of course they are purely mischievous. To counter them, we heard the new War Minister last night appeal for Local Defence Volunteers to deal with parachutists. That at least is something I can do. . . .'

Despite the two telegrams despatched to Chief Constables by the Under-Secretary of State at the Home Office, some sections of the police force seemed to be remarkably ill-informed of the situation in the immediate wake of Eden's broadcast. Alan Lawrie was another of the earliest volunteers. He went along with a friend to enrol at the police station in Cambridge on the morning of 15 May. 'The sergeant knew nothing of the Local Defence Volunteers. . . . However, he took our names and recorded them on the back of an envelope!'

Meanwhile, in Sussex early the same day the novelist and biographer Ernest Raymond was equally swift to answer the call. '. . . I confess I expected some praise for this promptitude. . . . It was not forthcoming. The uniformed policeman behind his desk sighed as he said "We can take your name and address, that's all." A detective-inspector in mufti, whom I knew, explained this absence of fervour. "You're about the hundred and fiftieth who's come in so far, Mr Raymond, and it's not yet half-past nine. Ten per cent of 'em may be some use to Mr Eden but, lor' luv-a-duck, we've had 'em stumping in more or less on crutches. One old codger who we knew for a cert is seventy-odd came in and swore he was sixty-one. I said "Make it sixty-two, Charlie," but he said, "No, sixty-one. Last birthday." And the kids! Gawd-aw'mighty, we've had 'em coming in and swearing they were seventeen last March. We've taken their names but, Gawd's truth, this is going to be Alexander's rag-time army". . . .'

Although, during the course of his broadcast, Eden had emphasised (by repeating several times) the age-range for those men who were eligible to enrol as Local Defence Volunteers, many – some no more than boys and others approaching their second childhood – simply ignored that stipulation and enrolled anyway, in a desperate bid for the welcome opportunity to 'do their bit'. Given that within a day or so of the War Minister's appeal nearly a quarter of a million men had signed up for service in the new civilian army it was hardly surprising that, for a dauntingly overstretched police force, the verification of potential volunteers' ages was something of a hit or miss affair. Sixteen year-old Norman Ford was a schoolboy in Bournemouth. 'I was an evacuee in a seaside town which could well have been a landing place for Hitler's invading army. . . . Most of the group I associated with could hardly

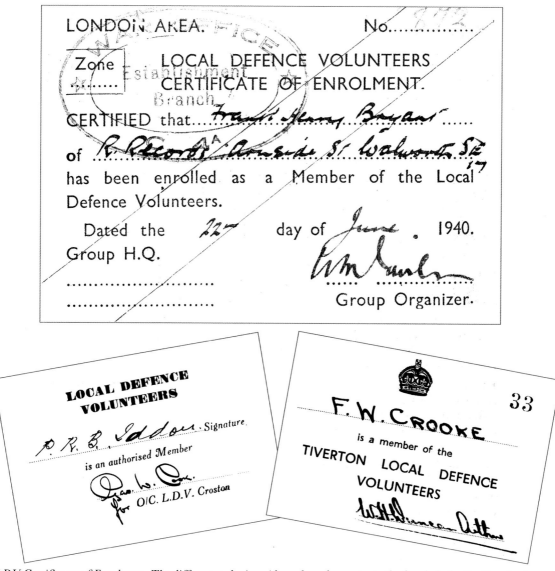

LDV Certificates of Enrolment. The different styles in evidence here demonstrate the force's lack of uniformity in its early days.

wait to join the new force, not so much to die for our island home but to combat the humiliation of looking old enough to serve while being treated like children and compelled to wear a school cap at all times. . . . So, when Eden's call came we did not seek official permission but enrolled next day at Boscombe drill-hall. No one questioned our ages. We were immediately accepted without reference to school or parents.'

Philip Longes enrolled at Surbiton, but his introduction to the LDV came about in a slightly different way. 'I was taking my usual evening stroll with my wife. . . . As we rounded the corner of a road and came to a stretch of open country consisting of a sports and recreation ground, a small procession hove into sight. It consisted of half a dozen men clad in a motley assortment of garments: old flannel trousers, gardening clothes, old mackintoshes. . . . One of the men in the procession [made] his way towards us. . . . He wanted to know if I lived locally, whether I was doing anything in the national effort and finally whether I would care to join his platoon of Local Defence Volunteers. He told me to give the matter my earnest consideration and, if I [decided] to join he would make arrangements for me to [be enrolled]. . . . The next evening I presented myself at the sports pavilion, which I found was the HQ of the local (Surbiton) company of the LDV, and I was duly taken by car with three other recruits to the Police Station to be sworn in. . . .'

No one could have possibly predicted the extent to which War Minister Eden's appeal for men to form a new civilian army to help defend the Home Front would catch the public imagination. One observer in Abingdon (then the county town of Berkshire but now in Oxfordshire) described what happened there. 'Men of all shapes and sizes literally flocked in. Veterans of the [last] war, considered too old for this one, ever eager to show there was "life in the old dog yet", and the middle-aged whose civilian occupation was of a character essential to the war effort, and lads of seventeen who were sure they could "put up a good show". The most elastic interpretation was put on the condition of "reasonable physical fitness".'

In the nearby village of Fyfield some of the 'regulars' at the White Hart Inn decided to take prompt action. 'A few of us were having a drink and discussing the war . . . when Mr Eden's call came for Local Defence Volunteers to defend Britain,' explained one of the pub's denizens. 'That night . . . after some talk it was decided to form a Fyfield and Tubney [a neighbouring village] platoon of the LDV. . . . It was fixed for a police sergeant from Cumnor to come to the White Hart and enrol members. A good number were enrolled and some time later formally sworn-in at Tubney School by Captain Cheshire, who was in charge of the [local] area.'

Everywhere in the country the reaction was the same. The War Minister had exactly caught the mood of the times and men up and down the land – those too old or too young for active service, and others of all ages who were in reserved occupations and therefore prevented from joining the Regular Forces – were more than eager to take up the opportunity that Eden had offered them. No wonder, then, that supplies of hastily-prepared enrolment forms soon proved to be inadequate, and that volunteers found themselves signing their names on odd slips of paper and the backs of envelopes. Just over four and a half years later, when the story of the Home Guard reached its wartime conclusion, King George VI, in a valedictory broadcast to members of the force, summed up those first chaotic days perfectly. 'Throughout Britain and Northern Ireland the nation answered [the] summons, as free men will always answer when freedom is in danger. From fields and hills, from factories and

Southern Railway employees – from clerks to engine drivers – volunteering for LDV service, May 1940.

mills, from shops and offices, men of every age and calling came forward to train themselves for battle. . . .'

Couching the same sentiment in slightly different terms, a patriotic Christmas card that was in circulation at the end of 1940 bore the following (entirely unseasonal) doggerel verse:

> The man who owns a mansion
> The chap who keeps a pub
> The tradesman, the mechanic
> The veteran, the cub
> The black coat office worker
> The toiler on the land
> And every other sort of bloke
> Has come to lend a hand.

CHAPTER 2

Look, Duck and Vanish

In the late spring of 1940, having observed the form of warfare that had been so successfully employed in Holland, Belgium and elsewhere in occupied Europe, the Government felt there was a real threat that German troops might be dropped in the remoter areas of Britain by parachute. The popular perception was that these invaders would land in disguise; dressed as policemen, perhaps, or air-raid wardens. Imagination ran riot, and people half expected to see Nazi paratroopers dropping from the sky kitted out even as nuns and choir boys! In his BBC broadcast of 14 May, Eden had outlined the purpose and consequences of these clandestine tactics. 'The troops are specially armed, equipped, and some of them have undergone specialised training. Their function is to seize important points such as aerodromes, power stations, villages, railway junctions and telephone exchanges – either for the purpose of destroying them at once or of holding them until the arrival of reinforcements. The purpose of the parachute attack is to disorganise and confuse, as a preparation for the landing of troops by aircraft.'

It was to help combat – and to reduce the possibility of – this form of enemy infiltration that the LDV was initially raised and so it was that, in this climate of urgency, many volunteers found themselves attending makeshift parades and even going out on patrol before the ink had properly dried on their applications. At the village of St Newlyn East near Newquay, Rex Davey, along with many other young men working on local farms or in other reserved occupations, together with those who were too old for military service, signed on to join the LDV on the evening of Eden's broadcast. 'Soon, "armed" with 12-bore shotguns, .22 rifles, pikes and pitchforks, we were given weekly night duties between 10 p.m. and 6 a.m. to guard the pool fuel depot at Quintrel Downs. A caravan was placed at the crossroads, where were were able to snatch some sleep with 2 hours on duty and 2 hours off. We also had to guard the Newquay Water Company's reservoir adjacent to the main road between Quintrel Downs and St Columb Road, some five hundred yards away. After coming off duty at 6 a.m., I changed into working attire and brought in the cows to start milking at 6.15 a.m.'

Jack Hand, '. . . fired with patriotism and being just seventeen . . .' had signed up at Selston Police Station, near Mansfield. Within forty-eight hours, and equipped only with a hedgestake, he was out on night duty with another new recruit, who '. . . turned out to be an ex-First World War naval commander, a gentleman indeed. We duly began our vigil, and before long noticed that Ma Cooke had left the lights on in her Church Lane shop. After a lot of wheezing and grunting Ma Cooke – a hefty lady in her 70s – rectified the matter but, on going into her shop the following day, she gave me a severe telling off for "waking me up at that time of night".'

Wilf Hodgson, then a twenty-year-old farmworker in Lincolnshire, had registered for military service but had not been accepted as he was in a reserved occupation. Instead he enrolled in the LDV after listening to Eden's broadcast. 'I saw this as a chance to do my bit in the defence of my country. Within twenty-four hours a meeting

LDVs were soon on duty all over the country watching and waiting, just like these two men (and their dog) on the South Downs in Sussex. (IWM)

had been arranged at the village hall and a Selection Committee was formed consisting of the local policeman, a retired Army Captain and a retired Sergeant Major. I had a fair bit of experience with a sporting gun . . . and I was duly enrolled. Within a few days the first parade was called. Everyone was keen to get on with the job, but the majority had no idea at all what would be expected of them. . . .'

Derek Bee was also in a reserved occupation and experiencing some difficulty in joining the RAF. While waiting for his application to be processed he heard Eden's broadcast and enrolled in the LDV near Preston the following day. 'Along with many others, I assembled in the playground of a local school where an ex-Army Captain of the 1914–18 war took it upon himself to assume command. . . . My section consisted of an industrialist, a fire loss assessor who was rather deaf, a farm labourer and myself, a Chartered Accountant.' Within a few days of signing up, they were keeping watch together for enemy parachutists, saboteurs and other suspicious characters. 'Our place of duty was situated on a high piece of land in the depths of the country. It was reached by a narrow lane much used by couples in motor cars for what were clearly not enemy activities.

'Twice a week the four of us met at dusk and kept watch until dawn. Our only weapons were a 12-bore shot gun without cartridges, and a crate of pint bottles of beer (the latter provided out of our own funds). . . . After a month or so a very small wooden hut, containing two wire mesh bunks, was erected and shift work introduced [but] during my two months of service with the LDV I never saw anything remotely suspicious. . . .'

Hugh Aitken signed on at the police station in Leighton Buzzard, Bedfordshire, after hearing Eden's appeal and swiftly became a member of the Billington LDV. 'Our main duty in those first days was to watch the surrounding

Posters sprang up on noticeboards everywhere urging those men who were eligible to join Britain's civilian army.

countryside from our dug-out at the top of Billington Hill in the village. This was a nightly patrol to guard against an enemy parachute drop in the vicinity. The RAF Central Signals Station was only a mile or two away from our position, and the MI6 Code and Cypher HQ at Bletchley Park was only seven miles distant. We patrolled for two hours followed by four hours off, and our sleeping quarters were an old gypsy-style caravan which was quite bug-ridden and needed to be fumigated from time to time. As it was, we frequently went off duty to do our daily work madly scratching ourselves! All we were issued with [at first] were an LDV armband and a wooden pole (about six feet in length) very similar to the 1930s' Boy Scouts' staff, and that was it!'

Alan Hollingsworth enrolled in Grimsby and two evenings later found himself attending his first parade of local members at one of the town's church halls. 'When we all gathered there for the first time . . . it was soon apparent that we all knew each other – as friends, neighbours and colleagues. There were three main groups: the veterans of the First World War, then mostly in their forties – they, of course, were the "Dads"; then there were the "in-betweens" – younger men who for the most part had no military experience but many of whom were in reserved occupations; and finally there were the recent school-leavers . . . who were waiting to be called up or to volunteer.'

Philip Longes had enrolled at Surbiton. 'We were a motley crew drawn from all classes of life. Clerks, commercial travellers, groundsmen, mechanics, shop assistants, bank clerks and secondary school boys all rubbed shoulders together. We were very correct in our attitude towards each other in those far off days; the surname prefixed by "Mr" was the common mode of address, and what we lacked in military knowledge and skill we more than made up for in dignity. For, after all, were we not volunteers and, as such, worthy of respect? . . . I do not think the atmosphere was very military, but we had this in common: we were a little band of brothers drawn together for the purpose of defending our neighbourhood from the threat of parachute troops and Fifth Columnists, and in this business we had at least a plentiful supply of enthusiasm.'

There was scant evidence in the early days and weeks of the LDV's existence of the weapons and uniforms with which the War Minister had promised to furnish volunteers. At first, nothing more than arm-bands bearing the printed initials LDV were issued to serve as a uniform, and weapons comprised hardly more than the motley collection of whatever volunteers could or, in many cases, could not bring along from home. The writers of the TV series *Dad's Army* exactly caught the flavour of the LDV's early weeks in this respect. Instructed by Captain Mainwaring – in the first episode – to attend their inaugural parade bearing whatever weapons were at their disposal, members of the fictional Walmington-on-Sea platoon assembled with hardly more than an umbrella, a yard broom and one gun between them. (A rota was to be drawn up for possession of the gun!). Here, truly, was a case of art reflecting life.

Philip Longes again: 'If "Jerry" had succeeded in setting foot on our territory, desperate indeed would have been our plight. Of course, we did not know then what we know now; but what use would sixty untrained men have been equipped with eight rifles, an ancient German Mauser rifle captured in the First World War, one shotgun, one revolver and a .22 miniature rifle, pitched against well armed and highly trained enemy troops?'

'Our weapons at that time were not impressive,' confirms Alan Lawrie, by now a newly-enrolled member of the nascent LDV at Grantchester on the outskirts of Cambridge. '. . . a couple of shotguns, a pitchfork or two, and later several pikes from the War Office. The latter might have impaled the occasional paratrooper but they were hardly the kind of thing to give one confidence. However, we found more satisfaction from the contribution of a local man who had hunted big game in Africa. As I remember it was a .405 elephant rifle, very heavy, with telescopic sights. It had one drawback. The donor could find only eighteen rounds of ammunition. The fact that the bullets were soft-nosed and against the Hague Convention did not worry us in the least. . . .'

Harry Hartill, who served in West Wales, recalls that in these early days '. . . our armaments were half a dozen rifles without firing pins, one Lewis gun which only two of us were permitted to fire, and a six-inch Howitzer which had probably seen service in the Boer War, and bore a brass plaque on the barrel saying 'Property of Birmingham Parks Committee'. This was what we had to defend Pembroke Dock with!'

George Beardmore, helping to guard the nerve-centre of the country's broadcasting system in London, sounded an uncompromisingly pessimistic tone in his diary entry for 9 June. '. . . we drill in the Concert Hall [of Broadcasting House] with broomsticks, have inspections in which the same unlucky fellow with long hair is repeatedly told to visit the barber's, and are likely to serve no useful purpose whatever should Germans appear in Upper Regent Street.'

Captain Warren Jenkins, historian of the 6th Battalion Monmouthshire Home Guard, succinctly summed up the position for many at this time. 'For arms – anything in the nature of a lethal weapon, safe or unsafe (generally unsafe). A few rifles, for the most part museum pieces, which on examination led one to speculate which end constituted the greater danger if anyone could be found foolish enough to fire them. Revolvers ancient and modern (chiefly ancient) and generally devoid of ammunition. Two of these latter proved to be a pair of duelling pistols, treasured probably from those far-off days when some distant ancestor of the donor formed part of another Home Guard, operating under very similar circumstances, facing another foe across the same Channel. . . .'

In the absence of proper uniforms and weapons, Local Defence Volunteers – a significant number of whom, except for veterans of the First World War and even earlier conflicts, were completely without any military experience or training – made a less than favourable impression at first sight. Dressed in civilian clothing and often wielding the strangest implements in lieu of real arms, the men soon became the butt of music-hall humour. Immediately latching on to the new force's initials, comedians quipped about the 'last desperate venture', 'long-dentured veterans' and, perhaps most famously of all, the 'look, duck and vanish brigade'.

In one sense the LDV was a victim of its own success. Enrolment numbers grew so quickly and to such vast proportions that even in peacetime conditions, let alone during the war when almost every item you could think of was in short supply, it would have been difficult to clothe and arm so many men at such short notice. In the prevailing circumstances of 1940 the task was manifestly an impossible one. As Major E.A. Mackay explained in his *History of the Wiltshire Home Guard*: 'Our beginnings were very humble. Headquarters of companies, platoons and even battalions were located in houses or rooms begged or borrowed, in stables, out-houses and bar parlours. . . . Later, accommodation was requisitioned and rooms were hired for offices, stores and training. Makeshift also were our look-out posts. Shepherds' vans were much in demand and others were made locally with boards and rabbit-netting. Our primitive road-blocks were things to look back at with a shudder. One dreads to think what would have been their fate if they had really been put to the test. . . .'

Graves quotes the detailed list of improvised equipment that was begged, borrowed or otherwise scrounged for use by one of the hard-pressed Wiltshire units. Included in the inventory were two shepherds' vans borrowed from local farmers and the body of a saloon car acquired from a nearby breaker's yard (all to serve as nocturnal shelters for the men on observation post duty); two ancient candle signalling lamps donated by 'a kind friend'; twelve signal flags; cable and old instruments 'scrounged by members from Heaven knows where'; an adjustable trip wire for motor cyclists made up of a clothes line and pulley; mufflers etc., knitted by wives and girlfriends.

'The amount of humble improvisation which went on . . . was staggering,' confirms Captain Simon Fine, in his 1943 publication *With the Home Guard*. 'I know of a company which supplied each of its sections with first-class bayonet standards and rifle-aiming rests from wood salvaged from scrap dumps. . . . The wood was transported free in the van of one of the [volunteers] who was in the haulage trade. All the carpentry was carried out by the men during their rest periods when they were on guard duty.'

Everywhere the position was the same. The LDV stood virtually alone and was almost completely starved of vital resources. Kenneth Harrop recalls his basic training at that time in the Stretford area of Manchester. 'We had no rifles, of course, and we had to use broom handles with which we lunged fiercely at straw-filled bags suspended on a rope from a frame. We certainly did not have any uniform for some time, and were given khaki armbands bearing the lettering LDV. Those were worn on the left arm of our workaday suits.'

This simple hut on wheels (seen behind the traction engine) was used as a guardroom–cum–rest quarters by the men of the Pinchbeck LDV near Spalding, Lincolnshire.

Bob Brown, along with a few other raw volunteers, found himself helping to guard a gasworks in Stretford on the very evening of the day that he had enrolled in the LDV. 'We were given a thick walking-stick as no weapons were being issued just then. . . . If the Germans had come that night what good could we have done with a walking-stick?'

It is hardly surprising that chaos, coupled with an awesome state of unpreparedness, reigned during the LDV's early weeks. The almost complete lack of bureaucracy which had preceded its creation was matched – at first, anyway – by an apparent lack of official organisation with which to quickly shape it into a coherent body and effective force. As matters turned out, these problems were to be overcome swiftly and effectively once the Home Guard (as the LDV was shortly to be known) developed closer links with the structure of the Regular Army.

Initially, however, a chain of command began, in effect, with the Lord Lieutenant of each county, to all of whom Eden had sent telegrams simultaneously with his broadcast of 14 May asking for their help and co-operation with the setting up of the LDV, '. . . as to which instructions have been issued to your local Military Authorities, including the Area [Army] Commanders who will be primarily concerned with the detailed arrangements.' This form of hierarchical structure turned out to be a somewhat haphazard affair, and was

Raw recruits to the Port of London Authority LDV. There is a good supply of weapons here but, except for the tin hats, few uniforms seem to have arrived. (IWM)

based to a large extent on harnessing the goodwill and expertise of retired army officers around the country to undertake the necessary – although frequently time-consuming and tedious – organisation and administration required to put in place suitable leaders at a local level. Graves paid tribue to these 'unfortunate Blimps' as he describes them; men who had hitherto been passing their twilight years with a little light gardening or following some other undemanding pursuit. Suddenly, they were landed with a hundred and one jobs all equally urgent: '. . . filling in enrolment forms, making card indexes with their own fair hands, shaking the men together, explaining to them what it was all about, going to the police station to collect twenty greasy rifles in their own car, distributing these, scraping up loose rounds of .303 ammunition, counting it out in tens and distributing it, collecting odd bits of clothing from the police station, visiting OPs [observation posts] every night . . .' and so on. The pace was relentless.

Keepers on London County Council commons and parks were trained as Local Defence Volunteers. A sergeant from the Regular Army instructs park-keepers in loading rifles during a training session held on a South London common. (IWM)

The somewhat confused state of the LDV's structure was made even more complex by the fact that, in addition to the countless units raised in villages, towns and cities throughout the land, a vast number of private companies, organisations and institutions had set up their own separate groups of LDVs. For example, the various private companies which operated Britain's labyrinthine rail network in those pre-nationalisation days, were extremely quick off the mark to recruit their own volunteers. At that time, the country was served by a network of main and branch railway lines extending over 20,000 miles, and it was estimated that, by the beginning of August 1940, over 100,000 railway employees had answered the call to protect the system from enemy attack. The Southern Railway alone enrolled 35,000 men, who were organised into six sections ranging from Kent to Devon, each section later becoming a battalion and forming part of the regiments of their respective counties.

Reflecting the legendary 'wartime spirit' that existed throughout the country, a new sense of 'pulling together' permeated the railway's workforce. However, human nature being what it is (even in wartime), this camaraderie was occasionally punctured by a lapse of good manners. A former Home Guard in Gloucestershire, whose duty it regularly was to keep vigil a few yards inside the entrance to Sapperton Tunnel on a stretch of the Great Western Railway, claimed that the driver of one particular train invariably let off steam as the engine approached the opening, on purpose to annoy him!

Volunteers at London's Stock Exchange being inspected on the world-famous 'floor' by Lieut Col T.W. Towers-Clark of the Coldstream Guards, August 1940. (IWM)

The boys of Eton College, one of England's most famous public schools, formed their own LDV Corps. Here they are being inspected outside the college gates on 21 June 1940. (IWM)

Every yard of Britain's 20,000 or so miles of main and branch railways was patrolled by company employees who were swift to join the railway's own sections of Britain's civilian army. (IWM)

An obviously choreographed scene showing three members of the railway's own Home Guard patrolling at a London terminus in the early hours of 30 July 1940. (IWM)

A group of Home Guards securing their observation post with sand-bags on the roof of an office block overlooking Tottenham Court Road in Central London.

Thinking back to those first days during a speech given in the House of Commons on 19 November 1940, Sir Edward Grigg (joint Under-Secretary of State for War responsible for overseeing the LDV) conceded that '. . . in the early stages . . . the system of command, the organisation and the administration were necessarily very largely provisional. The force grew like a mustard tree, and the administration had hard work in keeping up with it. . . .' As Norman Longmate observed in *The Real Dad's Army* (1974), even when the LDV's organisation was linked to the seven Army Commands into which the British Isles (excluding Ulster) were divided, '. . . at first many hardly knew what platoon they belonged to, let alone what battalion, and empire-building commanders were able to 'poach' whole sections from their less wide-awake neighbours.'

Meanwhile, all over the country in church halls, village halls, Territorial Army drill halls and whatever premises could be spared for the purpose, groups of eager LDVs met to be put through their paces in the rudiments of drill and to learn what this new civilian army expected of them. 'Yesterday the first drill of our platoon of the LDV,' noted George Orwell in his diary on 21 June. 'They were really admirable, only three or four in the whole lot (about sixty men) who were not old soldiers. Some officers who were there and had, I think, come to scoff were quite impressed.'

The initial purpose of the LDV was, on the face of it, straightforward enough: to report any suspicious or subversive activities and, above all, to keep watch for the landing of enemy parachutists. This inevitably led to more of the LDV's early nicknames, including 'parashooters', 'parashots' and even the ludicrous sounding 'parapotters'. (Local sobriquets along these lines were also applied here and there. On the Isle of Wight, for example, as Adrian Searle explains in his book *The Island at War* (1989), that famous nautical character Uffa Fox formed a unit of LDVs at the Medina boat-building yard which, as their leader, he promptly christened the 'Uffashots'). Guarding railway lines and equipment, communications systems, bridges, electricity sub-stations, water towers and any other sensitive installations that were at obvious risk from enemy action was also of paramount importance. Setting up makeshift road-blocks outside towns and villages in order to check the identity of all passers-by – motorists, cyclists and pedestrians alike – was another vital task. Road-blocks, it was to be hoped, would also have the effect of delaying Hitler's tanks should there be a land invasion by the German army. In fact, delaying and obstructing the

A pill-box on the banks of the Lydney Canal in Gloucestershire, photographed in 2000. It is just one of many around the country that survive to this day.

enemy by any means possible was at the heart of the LDV's *raison d'être*.

To help with this job of delay and defence, pill-boxes were erected around the country (some of which can still be seen today in various states of repair). In the event, these were used mainly as training posts and occasionally employed as ammunition and weapons stores. Many were ingeniously camouflaged, so that would-be invaders might remain in blissful ignorance of their whereabouts. Were an invasion to occur, however, the plan was that volunteers would man these pill-boxes and impede the enemy's progress by firing through slits cut into the walls of these makeshift strongholds.

'The tactical idea [of the Home Guard]', wrote George Orwell in 1941, 'is not so much to defeat an invader as to hold him up till the regular troops can get at him. It is not intended that the Home Guard shall manoeuvre in large numbers or over large areas. . . . The intention is that any invader who crosses any section of the country will always, until he reaches the sea coast, have innumerable small bands of enemies both behind and in front of him.'

Shep Yates's pithy analysis in A.G. Street's *From Dusk Till Dawn* (1945) could hardly be improved upon. '"We be a proper suicide squad, I reckon! Lookeezee, 'tes this way. Jerry'll come along from the coast wi' 'is tanks and all manner o' stuff. 'Ee'll beat up the Home Guard at Telmark, Sutton Evias, Hudwell, Bunchford, Willcombe, Chamton, and then maybe we in Wallop. But each village'll hinder he a bit. P'raps only ten minutes apiece. But six villages'll mean a full hour. Be that time 'tes to be hoped as the regular strikin'-force'll be got going, and 'it 'im fur zix."' The General Officer Commanding, Home Forces, not surprisingly chose to explain the position in a slightly different way. 'The two Forces [i.e. the Home Guard and the Regular Army], in my mind, are essentially complementary to each other; the Home Guard by its defensive, delaying and observing role, exercising a retarding action on hostile Forces which thus provides the necessary time to bring reserves of the Regular Army into play.'

Church towers – whose bells everywhere had fallen silent during the war, only to be rung to signal an invasion – quickly became the most favoured locations as observation posts. Almost invariably they offered unparalleled vantage points over the surrounding area from which to detect the possible descent of enemy parachutists or any other suspicious activity. The local vicar at Fordham, in Cambridgeshire, himself a member of the local Home Guard, is said to have provided a sack of herbal tea and a sack of carrots for the men taking part in these nocturnal vigils – the carrots were to enable them to see in the dark! Roy Rowberry, President of the still-functioning Leamington Home Guard Club, vividly recalls his spells of guard duty at Leamington Parish Church bell tower. 'The faithful verger, Willie Walton, let us in to sleep in the bell chamber and to climb out on to the "leads". I loved the dawn watch when with binoculars I'd scan the countryside. Half hopeful, half fearful of spotting descending Nazi paratroopers with jackboots dangling beneath nuns' habits; a disguise that popular wartime legend almost seemed to decree that they should wear! Church bells could then be legally rung, giving a warning of invasion.'

Meanwhile, in Sussex, Ernest Raymond positively relished his nights on guard duty during the weeks following the formation of the LDV. 'One of my section was none other than Christopher Stone, most celebrated of the early disc-jockeys. I used to like having him as my mate on the tower for a night watch, since he always arrived with a camp chair and a hamper packed with chicken and salad and sandwiches and cakes and bottles of wine – on a good night, champagne – that the length of the night might be made more tolerable. I remember tracts of the long night under the stars – never any rain that wonderful summer – when, instead of being behind my binoculars and sweeping the broad landscape for parachutists I was guiltily seated, shaking with laughter at his stories as I drank his wine or shared his chicken, while the rolling green fields of Sussex lay open to the enemy.'

Back on the ground (in more senses than one) Joseph O'Keefe, whose guard duty in those days comprised patrolling the hills overlooking Dunston near Gateshead, reflects the harsher side of serving in the LDV while at the same time holding down an arduous full-time job; a situation that so many men, except for the very oldest, found themselves in. 'We occupied what was probably a hen house. A couple of men would keep watch while the others would either sit talking or trying to doze until their turn came to go on watch. I remember doing a full day's work, getting my tea and linking up with the other members of the patrol. We would then make our way to the hills where we had a good view over Dunston and the surrounding areas. As dawn broke we would make our way back home, feeling very tired, to snatch a couple of hours' sleep. Then it was back to work for another shift. You certainly slept well the next night!'

At the other end of the country, just over the Devon border from Lyme Regis, C. Day Lewis had joined the Local Defence Volunteers at Musbury and was keeping vigil on another hillside, one which overlooked the Axe valley, where the future Poet Laureate waited

> For whatever may come to injure our countryside –
> Light-signals, parachutes, bombs, or sea-invaders.
> The moon looks over the hill's shoulder, and hope
> Mans the old ramparts of an English night.

Harold Richardson of Derby, who kept a diary of his service with the Home Guard, evokes the atmosphere of those long nights spent on duty. 'Our guardroom is the old club house on Markeaton golf course. . . . The shutters to the bar and the door leading to the old bottle store are firmly padlocked. . . . We have no electric light, only oil lamps and candles, and the heating is the responsibility of a smoky paraffin stove. Still, it's not too cold in here, and for those of us not out on patrol a battered kettle on the heater keeps us supplied with warmish water for making cocoa. . . . At one of the club room tables, circled in the yellow light of an oil lamp, [two of the men] shuffle a sheaf of papers and all the time confer in low tones as if reliving their own war of twenty years ago and planning some great strategy. Assorted grunts and snores come from a shadowed corner where part of our platoon, wrapped in greatcoats, lie on straw palliasses. Two candles, stuck in their own grease, light the table being used by a noisy pontoon school. . . .'

At Surbiton, where Philip Longes had joined what later became the 52nd Battalion Surrey Home Guard, a similar atmosphere prevailed. 'I, together with several other fellows, had sent my wife away to the country for safety and we, along with several of the younger volunteers, used to spend the evenings at our post and sleep the night there. We did this for two reasons: for companionship and to provide a reserve for the half section on duty. If extra guards had to be mounted or patrols made we were always available, and between us we presented the country with much of our spare time. The "garrison", both official and unofficial, had usually assembled by seven o'clock, by which time the "fun" up above was usually in full swing. Imagine a smallish room with about a dozen fellows in it. At the small table in the centre of the room would be seated perhaps four "crib" enthusiasts. Occupying the extreme end of the same table would be [two] others who played "shove halfpenny" for hours on end. At another table [someone else] was grappling with an attaché case full of office documents or writing a letter to his wife, while I

A senior pupil at Wellington College checks a visitor's Identity Card. Like Eton and other public schools, Wellington had been swift to establish its own LDV unit based on the college's Officer Training Corps.

hindered him by cleaning my rifle or equipment on the remaining piece of table.'

Large numbers of the volunteers who responded to Eden's appeal were involved at some stage during that late spring and summer of 1940 with the manning of road-blocks. Makeshift barricades sprang up all over the country designed to intercept potential spies and saboteurs, for it was widely believed that a Fifth Column was busily at work in Britain at that time. It was the LDV's job to hinder them and – if possible – to hand over all such enemy agents to the authorities. Although these obstacles were deemed indispensable to the nation's security, their presence in almost every village, town and city in the land became a source of considerable delay, irritation and, not least, danger to the genuine traveller. Bob Brown manned a road-block in Stretford. 'At each end of Crossford Bridge road-blocks had been placed to slow down the traffic and, in the case of invasion, to slow down enemy tanks. From about 7.30 p.m. till 6.30 a.m. our post would be manned by two men at each end of the bridge who halted vehicles (except buses), pedestrians and cyclists, and demanded to see everyone's Identity Cards. [Children under sixteen, incidentally, were not required to carry one]. In most cases the cards were produced and the travellers proceeded on their journey. There were a number of instances when cars were halted at a late hour and the occupants had no Identity Cards with them. They were nearly always younger people returning from a late-night party. We used to scare them about the cards and order them to report to Stretford Police Station the following day. Some of them probably did as we ordered, but we never checked up with the police ourselves.'

John Finn was a member of the Ramsgate LDV. 'My first guard duty, at the age of sixteen, was on a road-block in Pegwell village. There were six of us with

A demonstration, held in the grounds of the Home Guard training school at Osterley Park, showing the wrong way to stop the driver of a car at a road-block in order to examine the occupant's Identity Card. (IWM)

Members of the Southern Railway Home Guard at Dorking in Surrey learn how to erect a road-block speedily using blocks of granite and lengths of ironwork.

A waterborne 'road-block'. Members of the Upper Thames Patrol (see Chapter 7) stop holiday-makers on the river to examine their Identity Cards, July 1940. (IWM)

one rifle and about twenty rounds of ammunition between us. Our only uniform was an arm-band.'

Looking back to the LDV's early days in and around Rhymney, Monmouthshire, Captain Warren Jenkins acknowledged that '. . . road-blocks formed the focal point for all LDV activities. . . . [They] varied considerably both in style and dimensions. The smaller and less ambitious consisted of a few colliery trams and sandbagged positions, to the more elaborate variety composed of steel rails and concrete blocks. . . . Identity cards were examined, traffic brought to a standstill, any suspicious person interrogated, and all and sundry challenged until their right to remain at large had been established beyond doubt. Naturally, errors of judgement were committed. Sentries were raw, untrained in methods of challenging and of subsequent procedure. Some incidents were of a rather serious nature, but generally the goodwill prevailing at the time and a few words of explanation made all smooth.'

Captain Jenkins went on to describe how, in the tension of the moment, commonsense could sometimes become obscured during road-block checks, with situations occasionally developing into that of near farce. 'At Sirhowy, one evening, the [LDV] officer on duty arrived to find that, incarcerated in the Guard Room, were the greater portion of the local Fire Brigade. Tempers were somewhat frayed, words ran high, both sides were determined to uphold their rights. On the one hand, the members of the Brigade refused to supply means of identification, on the other the Sergeant-in-Charge denied to them their freedom until this had been done. Complete deadlock resulted, and continued until the arrival on the scene of the Deputy Chief of the Brigade. Identification was established and members of the Brigade departed.'

Writing in his book *The Phoney War* (1961), E.S. Turner explained the nub of the problem where road-blocks were concerned. 'Many of the [men] on road-block duty were trigger-happy, though not much more so than the Regular troops. Often the volunteers wore no identifying marks other than armlets and drivers mistook them, or professed to mistake them, for people seeking lifts. There were, as always, motorists temperamentally opposed to stopping in any circumstances. . . . These now found themselves running a gauntlet of fire, and so did deaf motorists and drivers of noisy vehicles. The result was a good deal of unnecessary work for the coroner. . . . The War Office was slow to prescribe and enforce an unmistakable signal for use at road-blocks, fearing that Fifth Columnists would employ it for their own purposes; but eventually it ordered that sentries should swing a red light when they wished to halt a car and not rely on a stationary red lamp and a shouted challenge.'

A Home Guard Instruction issued in November 1943 served to clarify for all concerned the correct method of halting cars. 'By day cars will be halted by ordinary police signals; by night a red lamp will be swung horizontally. The signals must always be perfectly clear and the man covering the block will not fire unless the occupants of the vehicle attempt to rush the block or interfere with the sentry.' Charles Graves reported that '. . . all over the country the LDV sentries and armed patrols ordered motor-cars to stop, and fired on them if they failed to pay attention to the not-always swinging red lamps which the LDV carried. More deaths occurred from this than from training in firearms. It seems that time and again an LDV when aiming at the rear tyre of a disobedient motor-car failed to allow for the kick of the rifle, and shot the driver or one of his passengers in the back of the head. . . .'

Manning observation posts and road-blocks, then, was the main task for members of the LDV during the late spring and summer of 1940, often – in the early weeks, at least – without the advantage of much in the way of uniforms or weapons, but with colossal enthusiasm and a determination to play their part to the full in Eden's new civilian army. By the end of June an astonishing one and a half million men had enrolled in the LDV, but before long, had they but known it, none of them would be members of the LDV at all.

CHAPTER 3
All the Bells in Paradise

In a memo dated 26 June 1940, Prime Minister Winston Churchill wrote to Eden: 'I don't think much of the name 'Local Defence Volunteers' for your very large new force. The word 'local' is uninspiring. Mr Herbert Morrison [Home Secretary] suggested to me today the title "Civil Guard" but I think "Home Guard" would be better. Don't hesitate to change on account of already having made armlets etc., if it is thought the title 'Home Guard' would be more compulsive.'

The following day Churchill sent a further note to his War Minister. 'I hope you like my suggestion of changing the name 'Local Defence Volunteers'. . . . I found everybody liked this in my tour yesterday.'

From that moment onwards the writing was clearly on the wall so far as the name Local Defence Volunteers was concerned, and on 23 July the title was officially altered to the Home Guard. Nobody could really deny that the new name had a better ring to it. 'Local Defence Volunteers' conveyed the impression of a force that was somehow quaint and amateurish; 'Home Guard' sounded definitely more businesslike.

However, if anyone believed that a simple change of name would prevent comedians from taking any further good-natured swipes at Britain's new civilian army then they were very much mistaken. Bridging the gap between the two titles, George Formby sang:

> I'm guarding the homes of the Home Guard,
> I'm guarding the Home Guard's home . . .
>
> One evening as an LDV
> Some German soldiers I did see,
> I ran like hell but they couldn't catch me . . .

Meanwhile, Robb Wilton delivered his famous radio sketch, 'The Day I Joined the Home Guard'; '. . . the missus looked at me and she said, "What are you supposed to be?" I said, "I'm one of the Home Guards." She said, "What are you supposed to do?" I said, "Supposed to do? I'm supposed to stop Hitler's army landing." She said, "What, you?" I said, "No, not me, there's Billy Brightside, Charlie Evans and Joe Battersbury. . . . We're on guard in a little hut behind the Dog and Pullet . . .".

In the fullness of time the Home Guard was to create such a place for itself in the nation's life and the public consciousness that even young children could be

Members of the Home Guard even had a railway engine named after them. This London Midland and Scottish locomotive was unveiled at a ceremony held at a London terminus on 30 July 1940. Lieut Gen Sir Henry Pownall (Inspector General of the Home Guard) did the honours. (IWM)

left in no doubt of its existence. Alison Uttley, in her famous and still popular Little Grey Rabbit series of books, published – in 1941 – a story called 'Hare Joins the Home Guard' in which the eponymous hero, wearing a saucepan for a helmet and wielding a catapult and toy pistol, set about repelling an invasion of weasels. There are no prizes for guessing who was in the author's mind as she described how these carnivorous quadrupeds marched along: 'Their teeth shone white, their noses were raised, and their little fierce eyes looked here and there, as their long thin bodies moved swiftly over the ground.' Needless to say, the weasels were soundly beaten and sent packing with cries of 'Courage! Fight for freedom!' ringing in their ears.

(There was a moment during the war when the Home Guard might have been the subject of a film co-written by the colourful Welsh poet Dylan Thomas. Julian Maclaren-Ross, all-round literary man and habitué of the pubs and drinking clubs scattered around London's Fitzrovia, was engaged by Strand Films to work on a documentary about the Home Guard in partnership with the future author of *Under Milk Wood* although, in fact, the script was never completed. 'It's hard to tell what the Ministry officials who'd commissioned it would have said had they seen the sequences we wrote,' confessed Maclaren-Ross. 'Neither of us having served in the Home Guard we'd had to invent our own . . . and what we concocted was a lively comedy-thriller set in a village "somewhere in England", stuffed full of eccentrics and containing a Fifth Column group, a delayed action bomb, and a German parachutist who'd been in civvy street a music-hall Master of Disguise.' One can see the effect that the pair were aiming at, but perhaps it is better that the project eventually foundered, leaving the Home Guard to be portrayed in a more appropriate fashion in such films as Alberto Cavalcanti's masterpiece *Went the Day Well*, based on a short story by Graham Greene.)

Churchill was quick to publicly press home the change of name to Home Guard in a speech. 'Behind the Regular Army we have more than a million of the LDV or, as they are much better called, the Home Guard. . . . We shall defend every village, every town, every city. . . .' Meanwhile, as Charles Graves pointed out, from Germany there was nothing but obvious contempt for Britain's civilian army. 'Churchill has spoken about Home Guards under arms,' observed a source close to Hitler. 'We ask under what arms? Broomsticks, or the arms of the local pub? . . .'

More significantly, the change from LDV to Home Guard heralded a new beginning for the force's organisation and command structure. In early August Home Guard units everywhere were linked to the Army's County Regiments, and within six months or so out went the old LDV titles such as Zone Commander, Platoon Commander, Volunteer etc., and in came the Army's ranks. Thus Volunteers eventually became Privates, presided over by Lance Corporals, Corporals, Sergeants and the rest.

Meanwhile, the almost surreal early days characterised by broomsticks and pitchforks had virtually drawn to a close as various, more orthodox weapons were made available for the Home Guard to use. In many instances these may not have been quite what in ideal circumstances the men would have chosen to be issued with. But, of course, the circumstances were far from ideal and, with so many arms having been left behind or destroyed on the other side of the Channel during the evacuation from Dunkirk, priority for the issue of the most up to date and effective equipment was naturally given to the Regular Army.

At Abingdon, 31 May proved to be a 'red letter day' for the men who were soon to become part of the First Berkshire Battalion Home Guard. On that date '. . . we received our first issue of rifles. The scale, it is true, was only about four per hundred men and ten rounds per rifle. Rifles which had been immersed in grease for a quarter of a century, and a very considerable amount of which was transferred to our clothes every time we handled them, in spite of the hours spent in vain efforts to remove it. However, the process of being armed had started, as had the howl for more – an importunity which was to last for many a month. . . .'

By the end of July, however, as weapons – including Canadian Ross and Lee Enfield rifles, Lewis guns, Vickers, Browning and sundry other types of firearms – trickled in for use by the Home Guard, courtesy of the War Office,

Members of the Home Guard were not paid as such for the time they spent on duty, although a meagre subsistence allowance was eventually implemented of 1s 6d for periods of continuous duty lasting more than five hours and 3s for over ten hours. (IWM)

so uniforms of a kind arrived as well. However, for most of the men the army's khaki battledress was something that would come later; in the meantime they would have to 'make do' (a concept that the Home Guard became well acquainted with through sheer necessity) with the denim overalls that were authorised for issue by the War Office. 'Those volunteers who had the experience of reporting for duty in the early days,' recalled N.R. Bishop, in his *Short History of the 8th Surrey (Reigate) Battalion Home Guard*, 'will remember how, on arrival at the guardrooms, each man took what he could from the piles of jackets and trousers, and adjusted them to his own measurements by dint of a great deal of struggling with pieces of string and other contrivances, not always with a successful result.

'Many a short man went to his appointed post with trousers much too long for him, producing a fine concertina effect, and many a tall man bore a strong resemblance to Will Hay's Old Boy, by wearing trousers like running shorts. And the danger of sloping arms displacing the string was a real and ever-present one. Proceeding "at the double" meant disaster!'

A.G. Street described what happened at Sedgebury Wallop (his mythical but typical south of England village). 'In the seclusion of the harness-room each member of the squad sorted over the twelve denim uniforms in the hope of finding one to fit, but with varying success. Shepherd Yates was the only really

```
                                        Form 8A
                    HOME GUARD
                SUBSISTENCE ALLOWANCE

     Rank
     Name      ..................................................

       Serial No........................

               Hours                              Amount
     Date   From    To        Duty          £   s.   d.



                                    TOTAL

     CERTIFIED that I incurred extra expense owing
     to duty, and claim subsistence as above under terms
        of A.C.I. 924, para 20 (b)—1940.
     Checked
```

(HMSO)

lucky man. When he had slipped his medal ribbons [on] he not only looked a soldier, but felt ready to prove it. But Goodridge and Lightnin' could do no better than battle-dress that enveloped them, while Walter Pocock had to be content with a blouse [i.e. tunic] and a cap, there being no pair of trousers large enough to contain his ample belly and posterior.'

Harold Richardson's experience will no doubt strike a familiar note with anyone who joined the force during the first few months of its existence. '. . . Tonight's parade turned out to be something of a farce – mainly because all the uniforms were of one size, extra large. The tops of the denim blouses hung down low so as to reveal our civvy ties and shirts of all colours and stripes. Some of us found that our blouses had no fasteners of any kind. These should have been press studs but none had been sent. And as for the trousers, there was no way of keeping these up without the aid of safety pins, all inches too wide at the waist and too long at the bottoms. Our forage caps, on the other hand, were all too small. This meant holding heads at an awkward angle to keep the caps in place. . . . Only the heavy army boots came in different sizes, and most got a pair that fitted. When the platoon stood in line for our first uniform parade we actually made our CO laugh. He said he had not seen anything better on the halls.'

The situation proved to be no different at Abingdon where, in mid-June, eleven pairs of trousers, eleven tunics, eleven caps, one hundred and twenty-one buttons, the same number of clips and eleven buckles arrived to clothe a unit of fifty-six men. 'Our triumph was short-lived,' explained one of the hopeful recipients, 'it soon being discovered that "suits" of denim was a misnomer, there being no relationship between a tunic and a pair of trousers marked with the same sizes. It was also apparent that we must all be either giants or midgets. In some instances it would have been appropriate to put the size of the collar on the trousers. Out of eleven suits, three men could be more or less reasonably attired. . . .'

Percy Nichols of East Sussex, who served with a Home Guard unit comprising Post Office engineers based at Faraday Building near St Paul's, explains how the disparity between a uniform and the size and build of its wearer could sometimes lead to faintly embarrassing

Home Guards like John Oxley, seen here at home in Northumberland, were proud to be photographed in their uniforms once they had been fully kitted out.

consequences. He was sent away to attend a brief training course clad in a set of ill-fitting denims. 'With denims, you needed to be either short and fat or tall and slim. Being neither of these, I could not obtain a set that was even an approximate fit. The trousers had no brace buttons and no belt loops. As there was no belt provided either, I had to tie them up with string! The itinerary for our last day included an assault course. All went well until towards the end, when we had to crawl under a tarpaulin, break cover, fix bayonets then charge and stab a dummy. I was halfway through my charge when the string holding up my trousers snapped and down they came in seconds, leaving me trying to hold them up while stabbing the dummy with my bayonet at the same time. Several visitors were present, including a number of ladies who were in fits of laughter at my predicament.'

As the long, hot summer of 1940 unfolded the Home Guard, despite these deficiencies in weapons and uniforms, slowly but surely broke free of its largely ramshackle origins as the LDV and settled into its established role all

Contingents of the local Home Guard marching to a Church Parade at St Keverne in Cornwall, at the end of September 1940. Some of the men are wearing uniforms although others are still dressed in civilian clothing. (IWM)

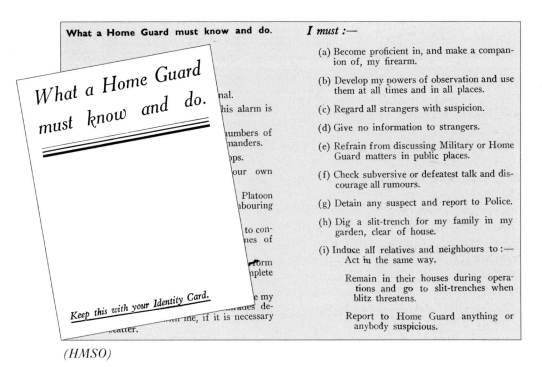

What a Home Guard must know and do.

What a Home Guard must know and do.

...nal.

...his alarm is

...umbers of
...manders.

...ops.

...our own

...Platoon
...hbouring

...to con-
...nes of

...orm
...mplete

...e my
...ades de-
...me, if it is necessary
...catter.

Keep this with your Identity Card.

I must :—

(a) Become proficient in, and make a companion of, my firearm.

(b) Develop my powers of observation and use them at all times and in all places.

(c) Regard all strangers with suspicion.

(d) Give no information to strangers.

(e) Refrain from discussing Military or Home Guard matters in public places.

(f) Check subversive or defeatest talk and discourage all rumours.

(g) Detain any suspect and report to Police.

(h) Dig a slit-trench for my family in my garden, clear of house.

(i) Induce all relatives and neighbours to :—
Act in the same way.

Remain in their houses during operations and go to slit-trenches when blitz threatens.

Report to Home Guard anything or anybody suspicious.

(HMSO)

over the country of watching, waiting and reporting while – from the middle of August – the Battle of Britain raged in the skies overhead. An official leaflet was issued to all members of the force, entitled 'What a Home Guard Must Know and Do'. It was to be kept with the holder's Identity Card at all times, and covered four closely-written pages. The formidable list of 'What I must know' included:

a. The Home Guard alarm signal
b. Where to report when this alarm is given
c. The address and telephone number of my Platoon Commander
d. The compass bearing from my post to nearby conspicuous landmarks
e. The rallying point to which I shall make my way . . . if it becomes necessary to scatter

The list of 'What I must do' included:

a. Become proficient in, and make a companion of, my firearm
b. Develop my powers of observation and use them at all times and in all places
c. Regard all strangers with suspicion
d. Give no information to strangers
e. Check subversive or defeatist talk and discourage all rumours
f. Induce all relatives and neighbours to report to the Home Guard anything or anybody suspicious

The inventory of 'What I must take with me when "Action Stations" is ordered' bears repetition in full:

Arms and ammunition
Full uniform and suitable underclothing
Steel helmet and cap
Haversack
Respirator, eye shields and anti-gas ointment
First Aid field dressings
Food for twenty-four hours
Knife, fork and spoon
Plate and drinking-mug
Water bottle
Pipe, tobacco, cigarettes, matches
Two handkerchiefs, towel, soap and razor
Money
Identity Card
Bicycle (with front and rear lamps), or any other means of transport ordered, in working condition
Corporals should, if possible, have a butcher's cleaver and a tin-opener
All other equipment for service in the field when issued

26

G.S. Publications

338

NOT TO BE PUBLISHED

The information given in this document is not to be communicated, either directly or indirectly, to the Press or to any person not holding an official position in His Majesty's Service.

HOME GUARD

INSTRUCTION No. 15—1940

COMMON GERMAN MILITARY EXPRESSIONS

English	German	Pronunciation
Halt ! Who goes there ?	Halt ! Wer da ?	HARLT. VAIR DAR ?
Hands up !	Hände hoch !	HENDER HOCH.
Come closer !	Kommt hierher !	KOMMT HEAR-HAIR
Surrender.	Ergebt euch	AIRGAYBT OICK.
Do not shoot.	Nicht schiessen	NICKT SHEESSEN.
Throw down your arms.	Waffen hinlegen.	VAFFEN HIN-LAYGEN.
Stand still.	Stehen bleiben.	SHTAYEN BLYBEN.
Go in front of me.	Vorausgehen.	FOR-OWSE-GAYEN.
Forward !	Vorwärts !	FOR-VAIRTS.
At once !	Sofort !	SOFORT.
Double !	Marsch ! Marsch !	MARSH MARSH.
Faster !	Schneller !	SHNELLAIR.
Slower !	Langsam !	LUNGSUM.
Left !	Links !	LINKS.
Right !	Rechts !	WRECHTS.
Stop !	Halt !	HARLT.
Come back !	Kommt zurück !	KOMMT TSOORICK.

NOTE.—The pronunciation given in Column 3 is the nearest English equivalent to the German sounds. The exact pronunciation can only be learned from a German speaker.

Prepared under the direction of
The Chief of the Imperial General Staff.

THE WAR OFFICE,
    20th September, 1940.

Printed under the Authority of HIS MAJESTY'S STATIONERY OFFICE
by William Clowes & Sons, Ltd., London and Beccles.

G. 254.—2438. (9/40). 180M.

Home Guard Instruction No. 15. (HMSO)

Local Defence Volunteers being taught the German translations of some brief but – in the circumstances – all-important English phrases.

On 20 September the War Office issued Home Guard Instruction No. 15, which comprised a list of common German military expressions and their pronunciation. (A note was added explaining that the exact pronunciation could only be learned from a German speaker!) The phrases rendered in English included, in the following order:

Halt! Who goes there?
Hands up!
Surrender
Do not shoot
Throw down your arms
Stand still
Go in front of me
Forward!
Faster!
Slower!
Stop!
Come back!

The final plaintive cries must surely have caused a ripple of amusement in the ranks and, at the same time, it might well have occurred to many members of the force that, with the gift of hindsight, this Instruction could usefully have been issued a few weeks earlier because, after several months on full-scale invasion alert, the Home Guard was called out all over the country during the evening and night of Saturday 7 September. Later dubbed 'Black Saturday' by Londoners, for whom it heralded the start of a relentless 'blitz' on the capital of several months' duration, many people on that day truly – though, as it turned out, erroneously – believed that a full-scale German invasion, in the form of a massive parachute drop followed by tank landings, was about to take place or actually even in progress. Eric Higgs was a member of the Lanlivery Platoon near Lostwithiel in Cornwall. 'On the night of Saturday 7 September the tides were right, the moon was right, the landing barges were in the harbours across the Channel together with a big concentration of German troops, and the military authorities believed that this was the beginning of an invasion. The day had witnessed the heaviest air raids so far over the airfields of southern England and over London. A preliminary invasion warning was given on the Saturday morning as the bombing began, and then as things worsened during the day the code word "Cromwell" was issued at 8 p.m. This meant that an invasion was imminent. I got the message about an hour later, and I can recall that night very clearly. There were just a few telephones in the parish at that time on odd farms, and a messenger arrived from a neighbouring farm to ours with the news from the Company's second-in-command that the code word "Cromwell" had been given. My task was to take my bicycle and hop over the fields to the next farm and to rouse that man, and so it went on throughout the parish. I would say that within half- to three-quarters of an hour we Home Guards had mustered at our road-block and had got it assembled. The road-block, on the A390 between St Blazey and Lostwithiel, was made up of railway sleepers and stretched halfway across the road leaving one side open. It was a very warm, quiet night. . . . Anyone who has been there in that situation can recall the feeling of the unknown, wondering what we are going to face. Of course, we were facing the best army in the world; the German army had swept right across Europe. I don't suppose – had the invaders come – that as Home Guards we would have stood a chance but, knowing the country, we could have delayed them for a while. The night dragged on . . . but it's peculiar how rumours get around. An army truck came down the road from the St Austell direction. The driver stopped, and we said to him, "Do you know anything?" "I've just come from Truro," he replied, "and I've heard rumours there that enemy troops are trying to get ashore at Marazion." Now, you see, this was nothing but rumour. Someone, somewhere had jumped the gun, and that was the sort of thing we were up against. We just didn't know what to think.'

Meanwhile in East Yorkshire, as John Ainley recalls, the men of the Nafferton Home Guard '. . . were hurriedly assembled, many having to be woken from their beds, and each sent to previously arranged posts. . . . For early September it was a cold but clear starlight night and the searchlights probing the skies over distant Hull could clearly be seen. Daylight came with a sense of relief that the night had passed quietly. . . . It later transpired that no thought had been given to a code word for "Stand To" rather than "Invasion Imminent" and it was the former that had been intended. Still it had served as an excellent but frightening exercise . . . although there was never again a call-out on that scale. . . .'

At Coningsby in Lincolnshire Wilf Hodgson's unit was called out at around midnight. 'The local village hall was commandeered. All members were issued with their various weapons and ammunition and ordered to man all observation posts and check points. I was detailed to set up a check point in the main street through our village and check every vehicle. . . .

'We stood to all night expecting any minute to hear the sound of aircraft or to get a message saying that the enemy had landed, but nothing happened and at 8 o'clock the next morning we were given the order to stand down.'

George Ames was a teenage Home Guard in Basingstoke. 'By this time I had been appointed the platoon "runner", which meant that it was my job [when there was an invasion alert] to go round on my bicycle and knock up the rest of the platoon members in their various houses. Inexplicably, some of the men seemed to lived right on the other side of town, which did not make my task any easier. When the church bells began to ring I accordingly set off on what proved to be quite an eventful journey. Any German parachutists who were about that night would certainly have had a hard time of it from the housewives of Basingstoke, let alone the Home Guard, because they were out in force with broomsticks, rolling-pins and all manner of domestic implements and improvised weapons, including axes used for chopping wood and lethal kitchen knives. I was knocked off my bicycle and threatened countless times by these enthusiastic ladies, but was offered cups of tea and showered with apologies once my identity was established. Given that I was riding about at midnight holding a large rifle their suspicions were understandable.

'I completed my mission successfully, but was quite appalled to discover that I must have lost the bolt of my rifle during one of these fierce attacks. I searched for it in vain, and dreaded having to break the news to our platoon sergeant who, when I told him what had happened, pointed out that now I had no means of firing my weapon I was reduced to the status of a mere pikeman. I had to give up my precious seven rounds of ammunition to someone else. . . . I was posted as a sentry outside the front door of our HQ with a fixed bayonet, where I would also be immediately available to jump on my bike again to deliver any messages if required. Thankfully we were stood down in due course and the events of that night declared a false alarm.'

Jane Uren was a child at the time, living in her grandfather's house at Camberley. He commanded the local Home Guard platoon and his house became their headquarters. Mrs Uren remembers '. . . lying in bed [on the night of 7 September] listening to the church bell tolling and wondering what would happen to us all now that the invasion had really begun. . . . My mother came up to my room and told me on no account to listen to any of the strategic planning that was going on downstairs. If I was going to be interrogated by the Germans I could not lie if I knew nothing. . . . We got almost no sleep that night and by morning we learned that it had been a false alarm.'

It was the ringing of church bells that night which many people remember most clearly. Silenced since the war began and only to be tolled to signal an invasion, the noise of them pealing here and there understandably caused much alarm and consternation, all of which only added to the general confusion.

A Home Guard exercise being conducted in the shadow of St Paul's Cathedral, amid the rubble of blitz-stricken London. (IWM)

William Collins of Sevenoaks recalls that he was on duty as usual patrolling a nearby stretch of railway line. Being close to London the sky, on that night of all nights, was filled with the sound of enemy aircraft. But oddly enough it was the church bells that made the biggest impression on him at the time. 'All the bells in Paradise seemed to ring out that night,' he recalls.

Widely mobilised throughout the length and breadth of the land, no doubt there was some sense of anti-climax – even of disappointment – among the Home Guard when the night's threatened invasion failed to materialise. However, it remains a matter of speculation as to what would have been the consequences for the men of Britain's civilian army had invaders turned up in full force at the Home Guard's road-blocks on that occasion. If only in that respect, at least, the night passed without incident (although it should be stressed that heavy bombing led to widespread destruction, death and injury) and, as Sunday dawned, it became generally apparent that this had simply been another invasion scare – albeit on the grandest scale to date – rather than the real thing. Home Guard units everywhere were informed that the threat of invasion had passed for the time being. The members of A.G. Street's rural platoon at Sedgebury Wallop were disgruntled, to say the least. "'Bain't 'em reely comin', Sir?" asked Tom Spicer wistfully, when he heard the sad news. "'Fraid not, Spicer," replied Walter, who by this time had hardly decided whether to be relieved or disappointed at the outcome of the alarm. "Jis wot I thought", growled Fred Bunce the blacksmith. "There ain't no dependence to be put in they Germans." "You're right there, Fred," chimed in Shep Yates. "I feared as much, an' it 'ave 'appened. The zods 'ave let us down proper. Yer we bin, 'anging about fur nigh on twelve hours, an' all fur nothin".'

The events of that weekend fell within a few days of the first anniversary of the outbreak of war. Eden, nearing the end of his tenure at the War Office, issued a message to the Home Guard marking the occasion. The force itself had still only been in existence for less than four months, but had moved forward considerably since its creation as the LDV. Doubtless designed to encourage and motivate, Eden's words must have bolstered the spirits of the men who, largely unsung and wholly unpaid, were voluntarily devoting so much of their time and energy to the defence of the Home Front. 'The duties of the Home Guard are many and various,' the War Minister declared, 'but however exacting these duties have been and wherever they have been performed, the same spirit of devotion and loyalty has been everywhere manifest. Already, during the intensive operations of the past weeks on the Home Front, the Home Guard has had opportunities to prove its capacity for service. The country has good reason to be grateful to the men who are devoting all the time that they can give to such an essential and patriotic service.'

CHAPTER 4

Playing at Soldiers?

As the summer of 1940 melted into autumn, and with the Battle of Britain won, the nation allowed itself a collective sigh of relief. The threat of invasion – although still very real – had receded to some extent from the heights it had reached in the wake of Dunkirk. Meanwhile, after the countrywide alert of 7/8 September, the Home Guard continued with its pattern of guarding and patrolling, observing and reporting, but now with an ever-increasing emphasis on training; something that would characterise the rest of the force's wartime existence.

The War Office issued a stream of Instructions detailing the subjects that should be covered in Home Guard training. These included map reading and fieldcraft, observation and reporting of information, familiarisation with possible enemy tactics, the recognition of enemy aircraft and troops, knowledge of first aid and elementary drill. During that first Home Guard winter of 1940/1, a great deal of useful information was imparted to the men on the ground through the simple expedients of training films, courses, lectures and demonstrations. It was all designed, as one early War Office training booklet explained, '. . . to keep alive the enthusiasm and corporate spirit of the Home Guard throughout the winter months when opportunities for collective training were few . . . .'

To cater for the not inconsiderable training needs of this still new but rapidly growing civilian army, a Home Guard training school was established in the grounds of Osterley Park, near Hounslow in Middlesex, during the summer of 1940. The property was owned by the Earl of Jersey, who was quite content for the Home Guard to use the grounds for their own purposes provided that great care was taken not to damage his magnificent house (a late sixteenth-century mansion built by Sir Thomas Gresham, founder of the London Royal Exchange, and completely transformed from the original two hundred years later by Robert Adam).

Privately organised and run by Tom Wintringham, together with a small staff of skilled instructors (several of whom, including Wintringham himself, were veterans of the Spanish Civil War), the Osterley Park training school rapidly acquired for itself a highly favourable reputation, and nearly five thousand officers and men from the Home Guard – attending weekend courses in many aspects of warfare including fieldcraft and camouflage techniques, guerilla tactics, the use of grenades, land-mines and anti-tank devices, street fighting, the use of weapons etc. – benefitted from the instructors' personal

A training exercise in progress at the Burwash Fieldcraft School, where members of the Home Guard were given instruction in camouflage techniques, making bivouacs out of groundsheets, cooking in the open-air and field sanitation. (IWM)

experience and expertise before the school was taken over by the War Office within just a few months of opening its doors for business. However, despite its obvious popularity, Osterley Park was the source of some official unease in government and military circles, largely arising from the left-wing backgrounds of some of the school's staff members and the effect this might have on what and how they taught. Some senior military figures were far from certain that Osterley Park was offering an appropriate syllabus, as George Orwell explained in a diary entry written shortly after the school opened, when he attended a lecture given by a very senior General who had been in the Army forty-one years. 'Dilating on the Home Guard being a static defence force, he said contemptuously and in a rather marked way that he saw no use in our practising to take cover, "crawling about on our stomachs" etc etc evidently as a hit at . . . Osterley Park . . . .'

Following the closure of Osterley Park, the War Office established a number of smaller schools – at Denbies on the edge of Dorking in Surrey, for example, and others at Amberley and Burwash in Sussex – all designed to cater for the Home Guard's training needs. Other schools that were developed along similar lines proliferated around the country, and a highly popular street fighting school was established in Birmingham. Graves explained the regime at Burwash. 'The principle of this school was to teach toughness and immediate reaction to the supposed proximity of the enemy. . . . Except in the depths of winter, the students have to bivouac in a wood. During the intensive course, lasting from Friday evenings to Sunday afternoons, they are taught how to kill enemy sentries silently, how to clear a wood, how to make personal camouflage and generally speaking how to conduct themselves as guerillas in a countryside already occupied by an invading army.'

Burwash spawned many imitators including, at Bletchingley for example, the school devised by officers of the 8th Surrey (Reigate) Battalion Home Guard, where the golf links were pressed into service for weekend courses in fieldcraft. N.R. Bishop, the Battalion's historian, records that, in these genteel surroundings, '. . . each weekend course culminated in a realistic exercise, in which the lessons of the course were put into practical effect. Live ammunition was then used, in order to inoculate the students with the realities of modern battle conditions. All the weapons available to the Home Guard, except sub-artillery, were employed at this climax to the course of instruction.'

A glimpse at the programme for the course held on 26/27 September 1942 gives some impression of the hectic and intensive nature of these occasions.

Saturday:

16.00–16.30	Arrive – Hand in ammunition – advance under cover
16.30–17.30	Introductory Talk
17.30–18.00	Tea for Party A, next period for Party B
18.00–19.30	Demonstration and Practice – Movement for Party A Tea for Party B
19.30–20.15	Preliminary Reconnaissance
20.15–20.45	Supper and rest for Party A, Cinema for Party B
21.00–21.30	Supper and rest for Party B, Cinema for Party A
21.45–22.45	Lecture and Demonstration Fieldcraft by Night
22.45–	Reconnaissance of Enemy Positions

Sunday

06.30–07.00	Reveille – Cleaning and Inspection of Rifles
07.00–08.30	Unarmed Action and P.T.
08.30–09.30	Breakfast
09.30–11.00	Exercise – Communications
11.00–13.00	Lecture/Demonstration/Practice – Camouflage Demonstration of Snipers' Suits
13.00–14.30	Lunch
14.30–15.30	Distance Demonstration
15.30–16.30	Stalking

16.30–17.00   Tea
17.00–20.00   Attack. Assemble at [given map reference]
20.00   Dismiss

Edgar Lister, who served in the Devonport Dockyard Battalion Home Guard, has memories of attending several training courses. 'There was one on maps and map reading which I remember in particular because, as an officer, I rated half a batman (one between two). On our first day we were taken out orienteering over a course which took us through some of the filthiest bogs and quagmires on Dartmoor. I finished up in utter despair, caked with mud up to the thighs. But next morning, Glory be! There was my uniform beside my cot, spotless, and my boots shining like black mirrors. I almost persuaded myself that I really was an officer and a gentleman! . . . Another course I remember for just one simple demonstration. The course was on camouflage and it was held in a big old house out in the wilds. The main point being made was that if you wish to remain inconspicuous, you must remain absolutely immobile. We were taken out on to the gravel drive, where the instructor said, "There is a brass button on the gravel. Can anyone see it?" Of course, nobody could. "NOW can you see it?" he asked again, and gave a twitch to the piece of cotton to which it was attached. We all did. It was such a simple demonstration, yet so perfectly effective.'

Away from the training schools, a number of booklets and pamphlets were issued, all designed to give the ordinary Home Guard some idea of his role coupled with no shortage of advice on how to play it. *General Knowledge for Home Guards* by Major G.S. Mackay ('late of the 7th Gurkha Rifles', as the title-page pointedly emphasised), was issued in the very early days of the force's existence, and consisted entirely of questions and answers grouped under such eye-catching headings as 'Brain Exercises', 'Appreciation of Situations', 'Intercommunication' etc. This pocket-sized book – designed to be carried around for frequent reference and priced at 1/6d – was published commercially by Pearsons; unlike other Home Guard literature which was usually issued under the aegis of GHQ Home Forces or the War Office.

Comprising seventy-odd small but closely printed pages, *General Knowledge for Home Guards* covered an immense amount of ground and was, according to its author, '. . . designed on the question and answer system so that it can be used as an aid and a refresher to volunteers whose aim is to remain proficient.' Any Home Guard who was able to answer even 50 per cent of the questions posed would have been proficient indeed. For example, questions in the 'Miscellaneous Knowledge' section included:

i.   How do you measure the width of a river?
ii.   When guarding or walking a prisoner, how do you stop him from bolting?
iii.   How can petrol be put out of action?
iv.   Who invented the Morse Code and when?
v.   When short of blankets how would you keep warm?

A.F.W. 4026.

Certificate of Proficiency
HOME GUARD

On arrival at the Training Establishment, Primary Training Centre or Recruit Training Centre, the holder must produce this Certificate at once for the officer commanding, together with Certificate A if gained in the Junior Training Corps or Army Cadet Force.

PART I. I hereby certify that (Rank)...Pte....(Name and initials) WOOLER R.P.
of HQ *Battery 24th Sussex *Regiment HOME GUARD, has qualified
   Company   Battalion
in the Proficiency Badge tests as laid down in the pamphlet "Qualifications for, and Conditions governing the Award of the Home Guard Proficiency Badges and Certificates" for the following subjects:—

	Subject	Date	Initials
1.	General knowledge (all candidates)	18.2.44	
2.	Rifle	18.2.44	
3.	36 M Grenade	18.2.44	
*4.	(a) Other weapon STEN	18.2.44	
	(b) Signalling		
*5.	(a) Battlecraft, (b) Coast Artillery, (c) Heavy A.A. Bty. work, (d) "Z" A.A. Battery work, (e) Bomb Disposal, (f) Watermanship, (g) M.T.	18.2.44	
*6.	(a) Map Reading, (b) Field works, (c) First Aid	18.2.44	

Date...12 MAY 1944...194....   Signature...gaulmee major...
                                           * President or Member of the Board.

Date.........................194....   Signature.............................
                                           * President or Member of the Board.

Date.........................194....   Signature.............................
                                           * President or Member of the Board.

Date.........................194....   Signature.............................
                                           * President or Member of the Board.

Date.........................194....   Signature.............................
                                           * President or Member of the Board.

PART II. I certify that (Rank) Pte. (Name and initials)...WOOLER R.P.
of HQ *Battery 24th Sussex *Regiment HOME GUARD, having duly passed
   Company   Battalion
the Proficiency tests in the subjects detailed above in accordance with the pamphlet and is hereby authorized to wear the Proficiency Badge as laid down in Regulations for the Home Guard, Vol. 1, 1942, para 41d.

Date...22 Jul...1944   Signature...K.Robertson...
                                Commanding COMMANDING
                                24TH SUSSEX (....) .....ION HOME GUARD.

PART III. If the holder joins H.M. Forces, his Company or equivalent Commander will record below any particulars which he considers useful in assessing the man's value on arrival at the T.E., P.T.C., R.T.C., e.g., service, rank, duties on which employed, power of leadership, etc.

Date.........................194....   Signature.............................
* Delete where not applicable.   O.C.

Home Guard Certificate of Proficiency which records various aspects of the holder's progress through the force.

A Home Guard exercise in Hyde Park. This lone figure suggests that the 'enemy' is either hiding behind the deck-chairs and lurking in the trees, or otherwise has simply gone home without informing anyone!

The book concludes by asking the question 'What is the Home Guard's job?' Despite its faintly patronising tone, the answer provided a useful working definition for rank and file members of the force to be guided by. 'Our first duty is to equip ourselves for any job we may be called upon to undertake, and for that purpose basic military training is all-important. The soldier who has a good grounding will automatically adapt himself as occasion demands. It's a bad spirit that prompts a man to say "That's not my job!" Home Guards just don't say it. "Generals Wanted", that well-known advertisement, means that the advertiser is looking for a servant who is prepared to do anything. In this sense Home Guards must be "generals" from the start. We are not Regulars, but we may be front line troops. Speed, therefore, must be our motto. Speed in thought and speed in action can only be achieved by sound training, and that military knowledge which alone will enable us to face any job with confidence.'

As time wore on, exercises – or 'schemes' as they were known – became a regular feature of the average Home Guard's weekend existence, with units devoting much of their energy to rehearsing the various methods of combat that would need to be employed should the enemy ever land on British soil. Mock

An 'enemy' parachutist being apprehended by the local Home Guard during training, and taken into custody by the local bobby.

A 'German' parachutist being searched after 'capture' during a Home Guard exercise held in north-west London, April 1943. (IWM)

A Home Guard exercise in Northamptonshire, 1941. Armoured 'invaders' have rushed one defence but they were clearly not expecting more problems from the little bush on the left. They surrender and are ruled out of the action. (IWM)

battles, for example, in which members of neighbouring platoons or companies would be pitched against each other (sometimes the 'enemy' was drawn from detachments of the Regular Army) were a frequent event. Certain strict conventions governed these occasions (the rules were enforced by an umpire, who was usually an officer) and if you were 'killed' during the proceedings you were honour bound to stay 'dead'. Apparently this was not always a disadvantage if your demise happened to coincide with pub opening hours! A former Home Guard recalls that, having been 'shot' during an exercise, he was making straight for his local hostelry when the Company Commander passed him. 'Are you dead, corporal?' the officer barked. 'Yes sir,' the man declared. 'I wish to hell I was,' came the heartfelt reply.

Francis Dancey, who was a member of the Home Guard in Northern Ireland, remembers the occasion when he attempted to circumnavigate this strictly adhered-to rule. 'Our company of Home Guard was affiliated to the Royal Ulster Rifles . . . [and] we had many exercises with them. They usually "attacked" our camp on Saturday nights. We had to try to repel them, but they always won because they were better trained and equipped and sometimes they roughed us up in the process. These battles sounded very real in the dark, with thunder-flashes, blanks and shouting. We wore helmets and they wore "head comforters" to distinguish each

Hand-to-hand combat between rival Home Guard platoons during a mock battle exercise at Alnwick, Northumberland. (IWM)

other, and the arrangement was that anyone who had been "killed" should take off his headgear and retire. Army referees were present to see fair play. One Saturday night we had an exercise and I got "killed" early on, and was told to take off my tin hat and go to the rear. I did as I was told, but I got fed up with looking on, so when I thought nobody was watching me I put on my helmet again and sneaked back into battle. However, I was seen and given a stern reprimand later.'

Rex Davey, who served with the 11th Cornwall (Newquay) Battalion Home Guard, recalls the very first exercise that he took part in when his unit, the Gummows Shop platoon, were instructed to 'attack and take' the Newquay Water Company reservoir which was being 'defended' by members of the Quintrel Downs platoon. 'As platoon sergeant, I was instructed to select twelve active men to mount the attack.

'At that time, on the farm, we had an old Chevrolet lorry with low sides and a well-worn engine with faulty ignition. At the appointed time I "armed" my team with potatoes as grenades and, as the men lay low on the lorry, we proceeded along the main road which ran adjacent to the reservoir. I was driving as fast as possible in bottom gear, with the engine revving and backfiring at the same time as numerous "grenades" were being thrown over the hedge at the "enemy". Having wiped them out we "took charge" of the reservoir. With the lorry loudly and continously backfiring, the "enemy" was beginning to think that an invasion had actually started!'

Members of the Wallasey Home Guard charge the 'enemy' while 'defending' the local gasworks during a mock invasion exercise, May 1942. (IWM)

It was inevitable that from time to time the Home Guard would find itself at odds with the local community. As proved to be the case in most other respects, members of the Home Guard were at a considerable disadvantage when they were training, compared with their near relations in the Regular Army. While the latter usually prepared for action in areas specially set aside for the purpose, Home Guard training was routinely conducted in town and city centres, suburban streets and parks, all in the full glare of public scrutiny. The uncharitable view expressed in some quarters that the Home Guard was merely 'playing at being soldiers' probably resulted, at least in part, from their high profile on these occasions. John Barfoot was a member of the Hurst platoon in Berkshire. 'On some weekends we held exercises in conjunction with neighbouring platoons such as Wokingham, Woodley and Twyford. On one of these occasions an incident occurred while on exercise with Twyford that could have come straight out of a script for *Dad's Army*. My section had instructions to go along the banks of the River Loddon to the railway bridge, to see if it was guarded. If so we were to drive off the guard, mount our own guard and the rest of us proceed to Twyford Mill. For this we were armed with replicas of Mills bombs made of clay, which dispersed with a small bang and a cloud of dust, and also crackers at the end of our rifles which operated by a string on the trigger guard. We decided to change our plan and approach from a different direction, as we would be expected along the river bank. As we neared the allotments alongside the railway, we could

The Home Guard defends a residential street with Tommy guns during a mock invasion exercise at Tilehurst, on the outskirts of Reading. (IWM)

see the guard of four men nonchalantly smoking under the bridge. We decided to cut across the allotments and surprise them. As soon as we started we were confronted by angry allotment holders, who told us in no uncertain terms that 'Digging for Victory' was more important than playing at being soldiers. Deciding that discretion was the better part of valour, we implemented Plan B. This involved going on to the railway embankment at the station and surprising the guard from above.

'As we tried to enter the station we were blocked by a ticket collector who demanded that we obtain platform tickets before setting foot on the platform. Putting on our best 'don't you know there's a war on?' attitude, we pushed past him and carried on along our way. The collector dashed over the steps to the stationmaster's office. This produced an enraged Mr Huggins [the stationmaster] shouting at us to get off his station. By now committed to the task in hand, we doubled back along the platform and mounted the embankment. Not to be outdone, Mr Huggins jumped down on to the line and followed us, gesticulating wildly. Reaching the bridge, we looked over the parapet and saw the guard still smoking and blissfully unaware of the drama unfolding above. Quickly dropping some bombs and firecrackers we surprised them, and they rapidly disappeared towards Twyford Mill. By this time Mr Huggins was getting near, so we scrambled down the embankment and, without placing our own guard, followed our Twyford colleagues as quickly as possible along the river bank. The result of

The Home Guard in Leicestershire captures a home-made 'Nazi' tank during an exercise. This heavily-posed photograph may have been designed for press publication or for use as publicity material. (IWM)

This home-made tank, built by the London County Council Home Guard, is a very different kettle of fish (compared with Leicestershire's effort), and rests on a Rolls Royce chassis, no less!

that day's exercise was: Stationmaster 1, Home Guard Nil!'

A natural over-enthusiasm, sometimes coupled with a lack of experience, was more often than not the cause of the problem when matters went awry during the course of these mock battles. Brian Cooper, who served alongside his father in the 7th Northamptonshire Battalion Home Guard at Wellingborough, recalls '. . . taking part in a war game involving the local Army unit. This was the Fife and Forfar yeomanry [an armoured unit stationed at Wellingborough].

My father had posted three of us behind a wall in the park near the centre of the town. We had been supplied with bags of french chalk, with orders to hurl them as simulated anti-tank grenades at any armoured vehicle which passed. An official umpire would then decide if we had in fact destroyed the vehicle.

As we waited we saw a small armoured scout car come down the hill, and to our delight the flap on the top of the vehicle was open. As it passed we hurled our bags of french chalk, two of which went straight through the flap and into the interior of the scout car. We were elated! The umpire was bound to give us a "scout car destroyed".

'Of course, the scout car came to an abrupt halt. But then to our amazement the head of an officer appeared through the flap, absolutely smothered in french chalk! His face was purple with rage and the umpire, who was nearby, advised us to retire as quickly as we could. Apparently we had "bombed" the Colonel of the Fife and Forfars on his way to a Church Parade [and] consequently he had been dressed in his best uniform. . . . Needless to say, he didn't get to the parade!'

John Slawson of Heywood, Lancashire, recalls that bags of flour were also widely used to simulate hand grenades, in his case '. . . plain for the "friendly" troops and self-raising for the "enemy". I well remember Magdala Street looking like a chaotic baker's convention after one such battle. I remember too one resident of that street asking if we'd nothing better to do than waste good flour when there was a war on!'

Arthur Meen was a member of the Home Guard at Wendling in Norfolk. 'An unforgettable incident involved the Regular Army playing the "enemy" and the Home Guard "defending" Wendling village against attack. Several members of Wendling's Home Guard were positioned outside the village to warn of the approaching "enemy", the object being to send up a flare as soon as the "enemy" passed the sentry.

Red Cross nurses attend Home Guard 'casualties' at a first aid post during a mock battle in the City of London. While adding to the realism of the exercise, the nurses themselves were also receiving invaluable training 'in the field'. (IWM)

'I was a sentry on the Swaffham side of the village and "enemy" Bren gun carriers passed my position on their way to Wendling. I tried to light a warning flare by striking it against a matchbox, but the flare stubbornly refused to ignite. I know now, but didn't then, that the flare would only light when rubbed against a safety matchbox. So I got on my bicycle and pedalled for all I was worth to reach the village via the back lane before the "enemy" arrived. Unfortunately, when rounding a sharp bend at speed, I ran straight into one of the Bren gun carriers and was immediately taken prisoner. My bike was hidden in a roadside hedge and I was taken in the carrier, and so had a first-hand view of the Army's "attack" on Wendling. As we drove towards the village I was being fired on with blank ammunition by my Home Guard pals, who were unaware that I was inside the carrier. They were hidden, or so they thought, behind trees and bushes, but I could see them clearly from my position with the soldiers. I'd previously given the soldiers a few seconds' worry when they thought the flare in my pocket was a bomb, but I was fully repaid when they went off to attack their next objective. They took me about four miles away and then let me out of their carrier to walk dejectedly all the way back to Wendling, where I had some explaining to do. . . .'

Charles Harrison worked for London Midland and Scottish Railways at Victoria Station, Manchester, and answered his company's call to join the Home Guard. 'The highlight of my "career" was a Sunday morning exercise, when the platoon to which I was attached had to "defend" Manchester Victoria station against an "enemy" made up of Canadian soldiers. Being splattered with red dye was the agreed signal that you had been "shot" and were therefore out of action. It was a matter of great pride to my platoon that in no time at all the "enemy" had been defeated and we were victorious. However, our elation did not last long. Ale was in short supply at that time and, unknown to us, Boddington's Brewery, which was situated just behind Manchester Victoria Station, had agreed to supply the local pub with an extra ration of beer for refreshments at the end of the mock battle. We then realised why all the Canadians had managed to be "shot" so easily. When we caught up with them we found that they were already comfortably seated in the pub, taking full advantage of the extra beer ration!'

Although these accounts dwell on the more light-hearted moments of Home Guard training – people inevitably tend to recall those occasions when plans went wrong or when an amusing incident occurred – the purpose of these mock battles was deadly serious. Played out in addition to the weekly commitment of parades and patrols, these often strenuous training sessions were yet another drain on every Home Guard's precious free time. Life was considerably tougher for most members of the Home Guard than perhaps many people today realise. Sympathetic work practices that are commonplace now were undreamt of during the war, so that few – if any – men who were in full-time employment (and that was the vast majority of the Home Guard) enjoyed such familiar advantages as days off in lieu or 'facility time' to help them cope with their Home Guard commitments. The son of a former Home Guard on the Isle of Thanet relates an all-too familiar story. 'My father and his brother were both herdsmen. They started milking by hand at 4 a.m. each day, seven days a week, and finished at 8 a.m. Then they prepared the animals' food for later that day, before getting home at about 11 a.m. They returned to work at 1 p.m. and finished at about 5.30 p.m. Their working day stretched over nearly fourteen hours and, during the summer months, they also made further checks on the animals in the evening. They had one half-day off per week plus a few hours on Sunday morning. On top of all this they would attend religiously for their Home Guard duties.'

Rex Davey also worked on the land. 'I remember the year that the LDV started we were harvesting wheat, and that's a heavy job. We'd finish pitching wheat at 9 o'clock at night and then home for a meal, a bath, and then Home Guard duty all night until we came off duty at 6 a.m., and then I'd bring the cows in and carry on right through the next day. . . . It was tough going, I can tell you, and then at weekends we were training all day on Sunday.'

N.R. Bishop speaks for the Home Guard everywhere when recalling the exertions of the 8th Surrey (Reigate) Battalion. 'If anyone is tempted to make light of their efforts . . . let him try the experiment of starting after dark from, let us say, Woodhatch, on a moonless night when the rain is falling and a chilling

Home Guard training could take various forms. These active members of the force are scaling the rocks of 3,000 feet high Tryfan. It is said this is one of the greatest and most dangerous climbs in North Wales. (IWM)

Members of the Home Guard (and spectators) relaxing during an exercise on the South Downs in Sussex. (IWM)

The end of a long day. Men of the North Lindsey Battalion Home Guard enjoy a rest and a smoke after a mock battle in North Lincolnshire. (IWM)

wind blowing across the countryside. Let him make his way, carrying military equipment, in total darkness over fields and across ditches, finding convenient breaks in hedges, stumbling in ruts, or disentangling himself from bushes; making his way with the maximum of speed into the bargain. Let him then try to penetrate the barbed wire defences of the River Mole and its tributaries in the inky darkness, and to ford the water itself. Then let him stand in those dank pill-boxes for hours with all senses strained to catch the sound of hidden approach by the "enemy". Let him attempt this sort of thing at the close of his daily work, getting back finally to his home in the early hours of the morning, cold, damp and utterly weary, to find a few hours' rest before he must start again on his civilian work. Then multiply the procedure night after night, week after week and month after month. . . .'

In general these extra demands were met with, if not always overt enthusiasm then certainly equanimity, and with the knowledge that it was all in a good cause. The experience of the 13th Staffordshire (Cannock) Battalion Home Guard is probably fairly typical. 'Taken all the way through, both before and after training became compulsory, the attendance on training parades was good, and for important exercises the percentage of men turning out was always exceptionally high. Inevitably, as time went on and the threat of invasion to this country became more remote, there were some backsliders, either by reason of long or awkward working hours, health or just pure disinclination. . . .'

Roy Elmer of Windsor believes that it was all valuable experience for the future. 'I am quite certain that Home Guard training served me very well, because when I joined the real Army I was far ahead of those who had not been members [of the Home Guard] in knowledge of arms and discipline. It might have been a joke at times, but there's no doubt that the volunteers were genuine in their desire to defend their land.'

CHAPTER 5

Arms and the Men

The Home Guard training programme laid a great deal of emphasis on the handling and use of weapons. The uninspiring sight of men attending for parade or going out on duty wielding nothing more threatening than pitch-forks, broom handles and other inadequate arms was of mercifully short duration and largely confined to the early days of the LDV. Following this poor start, however, firearms flowed into the Home Guard's armoury from across the Atlantic and also from sources closer to home. The items in question could not always be described as cutting edge or state-of-the-art, but they were welcome nevertheless. Canadian Ross and Remington rifles from America, Lee Enfields, Thompson and Browning machine guns, Vickers, Lewis and Sten guns were just a selection of the almost random assortment of firearms which eventually fell into the hands of the Home Guard. Training in the use of these weapons involved not only loading and firing, but also stripping them down and painstakingly putting them together again piece by piece. Ron Davey, for example, who was a member of the Tiverton Home Guard, recalls that he had '. . . to learn to dismantle and assemble blindfold' his Browning machine gun.

As the Revd Fred Beddow of Shrewsbury suggests, weapons handling for the Home Guard novice could prove to be something of a steep learning curve. 'We were shown how to use the Thompson machine gun but never issued with it. Instead we had the Sten. The first Stens were said to cost only 9*d* to make, and I believe it! They consisted entirely of roughish metal welded together and the only machined parts were the barrel and the bolt. (It showed.) But it worked, and that was what counted. Some care was needed because there was inadequate provision to disperse the heat generated by firing; also the ejection hole on the side of the barrel was unprotected and situated just where your hand would hold the gun. I suspect that I was not the only person to trap a finger in it as the bolt moved forward. It hurt but you only did it once!'

Those many members of the Home Guard who had seen service in the First World War possessed a solid foundation of knowledge and discipline which served them in good stead when it came to handling and using firearms during their Home Guard training. But it was inevitable that some less experienced members of the force, either owing to a lack of knowledge or care or because of a lapse in concentration, would occasionally run into difficulties. Frank Buckley, who served in a platoon near Oldham, explains how, during one training session when their sergeant was demonstrating the loading and unloading procedure for a .303

Members of the Home Guard in Essex undergoing rifle practice.

rifle, one of the men failed to eject all five of the cartridges before pointing his rifle upwards and pulling the trigger to check that his weapon was ready for loading again. As the men were undergoing this training in the small, dimly-lit factory which served as their headquaters, '. . . the inevitable result [was] that when he pointed his rifle skywards and pulled the trigger, bullet No. 5 made its exist through the roof . . . [resulting in] debris on the floor, a hole in the roof and a wrecked 100 watt bulb.'

A range of bombs and missiles, of which the 'Molotov Cocktail' is probably the best-remembered alongside others such as the aptly-named 'jam tin bomb', 'thermos bomb' and the execrable 'sticky bomb', have all become the stuff of Home Guard legend and at one time were widely used in Home Guard training. Edgar Lister vividly recalls the 'sticky bomb', which was a much feared (by members of the Home Guard, at least) anti-tank device. 'It consisted of a ball of high explosive, about five or six inches in diameter, wrapped in a coarse hessian material impregnated with an intensely sticky substance. This, in turn, was covered with a skin of some sort to make it possible to handle. The fuse was separate, and had to be screwed into a socket on the outside of the bomb. To use the bomb you had to peel off the outer skin then, carrying it by the fuse which doubled as a handle, you smashed the ball of explosive against some vulnerable part of the tank, where it would hopefully stick. You were told you should then walk quickly away, NOT RUN.' Mr Lister recalls one training exercise in particular at Devonport, when '. . . the Admiralty came up with a large sheet of

A sergeant from the Regular Army shows a group of Civil Service LDVs the correct way of handling their rifles. (IWM)

Members of the Ministry of Supply Home Guard in London undergoing firing practice with Lewis guns on the ranges at Wormwood Scrubs. (IWM)

'Molotov Cocktails', hand-grenades, gelignite and dynamite are among the exhibits of home-made items on display here at the Home Guard training school at Osterley Park. (IWM)

Regular soldiers in Liverpool demonstrating to members of the city's Home Guard how to destroy a tank using 'Molotov cocktails'. (IWM)

Members of the Ulster Home Guard in North Belfast being shown a petrol bomb. (IWM)

thick armour plating, the idea being that a select few of us would plant a sticky bomb on the sheet (which was lying on the ground) and retire in good order – we hoped! The first three or four went off satisfactorily, then the jinx struck. One refused to explode. The officer in charge had a problem. . . . He decided to send the next man up and get him to plant his bomb actually touching the "dud". His theory was that the second bomb would set off the first one by "sympathetic detonation". The second bomb failed to explode (possibly we had struck some faulty fuses), and the next man was sent to place a third bomb . . . making, at a guess, at least twelve pounds of potentially lethal high explosive. . . .

'The officer announced that he was going to destroy the bombs with an explosive charge. Luckily it was a success but, by gum, they must have heard the bang and felt the shock-wave in Tavistock!'

The Home Guard possessed two weapons, each of them highly whimsical contraptions, whose names and appearance suggest that they might have been more comfortably employed in the rough-and-tumble of the English Civil War rather than being engaged in Britain's mighty struggle with Hitler's Germany. The first to arrive of this inauspicious pair was the Northover Projector. Named after its inventor, Home Guard officer Major H. Northover, this hollow metal tube resting on a tripod was quickly dubbed a 'drainpipe on legs'. Equipped to fire a variety of grenades, it was basically designed to act as a short-range anti-tank weapon, and around 8,000 Northover Projectors were in service with the Home Guard by the summer of 1941. Many units were able to enhance the

Original cartoon by G.B. Rogers.

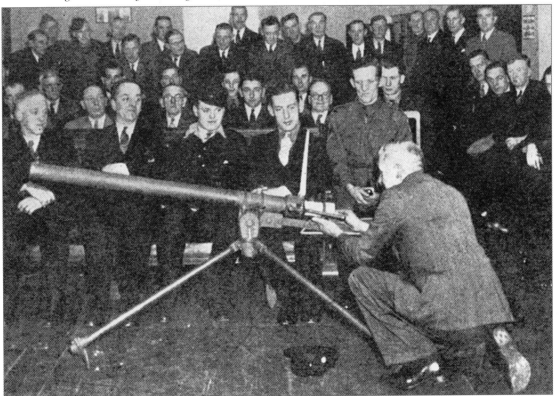

Members of the Southern Railway Home Guard attend a lecture on the Northover Projector at Waterloo in London.

Members of the Home Guard at Southwick in Sussex used this home-made trailer to carry a Northover Projector or machine-gun. (IWM)

A home-made artillery piece carried on a trailer drawn by a member of the 8th London (Royal Fusiliers) Battalion Home Guard. This photograph was taken in Conway Street just south of Fitzroy Square (part of the area covered by the 8th Battalion).

A demonstration of the Spigot Mortar (Blacker Bombard) given by members of the 2nd Southern Railway (25th Sussex) Battalion Home Guard.

Northover's mobility in training by ferrying the weapon from one location to another in small home-made trailers that could be hitched to the back of a car or even hauled along by hand.

The 10th Wiltshire Battalion Home Guard received a consignment of Northover Projectors on 7 September 1941. 'We think these much-maligned drainpipes . . . are quite useful weapons. They were issued originally for throwing Self-Igniting Phosphorous grenades. Sometimes they did and sometimes they did not, and not infrequently the bottle of phosphorous burst in the barrel. . . .' John Burt recalls how, one Sunday, '. . . we were on Scarborough Racecourse with our Northover Projectors. There were ten or twelve lined up six feet apart, like cannons at the Battle of Waterloo, firing rubber bottles at a Churchill tank that was running up and down.'

The Blacker Bombard (more commonly known as the Spigot Mortar) was an even more eccentric piece of apparatus. Again named after its inventor, Lt Col L.V.S. Blacker, this weapon could – in theory, at least – fire a 14lb bomb in the region of 800 yards and a 20lb bomb just over half that distance. It was described in a document issued from GHQ Home Forces as the '. . . most destructive of the Home Guard anti-tank weapons. . . . A direct hit will almost certainly severely damage, if not destroy, any heavy tank now known.'

Opinions about the accuracy of the Spigot Mortar in training differ considerably. (This was the weapon, after all, that was widely reported to have almost killed General de Gaulle during an early demonstration of its powers!). By January 1942, the 10th Wiltshire Battalion Home Guard possessed thirty-eight Spigot Mortars. 'Although at the beginning it was unpopular,' records the Battalion's historian, 'it rapidly became popular and was found to be a very accurate weapon that could be relied on. . . .' Undoubtedly the Spigot Mortar was more cumbersome than the Northover Projector, and many of those people who came into direct contact with it did indeed have reservations about the weapon's accuracy. Eric Gregory of Tamworth, for example, felt '. . . the problem was that [the Spigot Mortar] was so unpredictable that in order to be sure of hitting anything you had to be within about ten feet of it, and then the target had to be as big as a house! We pointed out that we did not think German tanks would let us get that close in order to have a chance of hitting [them].'

Some members of the Home Guard were killed and many others were injured in the course of weapons training; some during shooting practice on firing ranges and others when retrieving unexploded ammunition during exercises, or when the devices they were handling proved faulty and ignited prematurely. Robert Barnard was a young Home Guard at Barking on the eastern outskirts of London. 'Our rifle range was short and located among the heaps of coal and ash that surrounded the power station. Many Home Guards were poor shots – even gun-shy – and ill-aimed rounds were not always stopped by the ash heaps. At one Sunday morning range practice, before firing commenced, a private had been posted as a guard to stop passers-by from wandering into the danger area. He was hit in the abdomen by a bullet that ricocheted and he bled to death before anyone discovered his plight.'

Edward Down of Middlesex was killed during bombing practice, when a grenade fell short of its target. 'I take the view that he gave his life in the service of his country, just the same as if he had been on active service overseas,' commented the Coroner at the subsequent inquest into Corporal Down's death.

These are just two examples of the 1,200 or so Home Guards throughout the country who were killed by one means or another in the line of duty. It is a sobering statistic, and one which may well shock many people whose only knowledge of the Home Guard has been gleaned from episodes of *Dad's Army*.

CHAPTER 6

Shoot Them Down Yourself

There is still a widely held – but entirely erroneous – belief that the Home Guard was never ultimately tried and tested in battle; that throughout the four and a half years of its wartime existence none of its members actually came into direct contact with the enemy, beyond taking into custody the occasional German pilot or aircrew who had baled out in action and had lived to tell the tale. This misconception is understandable because, as it turned out, Britain (with the exception of the Channel Islands) was at no stage invaded during the war and the Home Guard was exactly what its title suggests: a domestic defence force whose members were not sent overseas.

However, for one quite substantial section of the Home Guard, nothing could be further from the truth than to suggest that its members were not actively and directly engaged in the conflict. By the spring of 1944, more than 100,000 Home Guards – some estimates put the figure as high as 140,000 – were working on anti-aircraft batteries throughout the length and breadth of the country and, in the process, relieving members of the Regular Army for service abroad. Many of those who were deployed on the gun sites may well have responded to a poster campaign which had been mounted by the Government in 1942, inviting men to 'Shoot them down yourself. Join the anti-aircraft Home Guard'. At first, it was left to the members of the Home Guard themselves to volunteer for duty with the anti-aircraft batteries, but subsequently a large number of men were transferred to these units from their existing battalions.

Edward Smith was just fifteen (although he had claimed to be eighteen) when he enrolled in the Home Guard. Within six weeks he had been trained as a gunner, and was assigned to an anti-aircraft battery situated on the outskirts of East London at Wanstead Flats. 'Our uniforms were slightly different from the normal Home Guard uniform and we wore the anti-aircraft insignia, which was a red square with a bow and arrow. Because of that we were known as the bow and arrow squad of the pikestaff army, but we took it all in good part. . . . We would go on duty from 8 o'clock in the evening until 6 o'clock the following morning on every eighth night. This was known as "manning" night and, in addition, we trained one night in eight. Each battery consisted of four troops, one of whom never actually manned the guns but did all the menial tasks such as preparing meals and cleaning and assembling ammunition, together with whatever else was required. Thus one

The 102nd Cheshire Battalion Home Guard Anti-Aircraft Rocket Battery, seen here in action, was formed in March 1942 on the Wirral as a part of the defence of Merseyside.

quarter of the guns were not officially manned, but anyone on site when the alarm sounded would immediately rush out and jump on those guns, whoever they were!'

Tom Murray was assigned to one of the anti-aircraft batteries which defended the city of Coventry. 'Our battery consisted of sixty projectors divided into four straight rows. Behind each projector was its magazine – a short, corrugated iron, semi-circular tunnel rather like a small Nissen hut, with a heavy tarpaulin covering each end. The rockets were stored inside on racks and were accessible from either end of the store. . . . Each projector could launch two missiles simultaneously from a double pair of rails and was manned by two men designated No. 1 and No. 2. The Battery Commander was a Regular Army major, who had a small contingent of Regular soldiers [including a] sergeant and corporal. These two were responsible for training and drilling the Home Guard. The corporal was a classic example of a traditional army martinet who made no distinction or allowance for the youth or age of his charges, or for the fact that we were at work during the day and soldiers for all of one night a week plus Sunday mornings!

'The Home Guard men were divided into seven "relief" crews, mine being No. 7 Relief, which meant that we were on duty on Saturday night. Naturally, this was the least popular duty among the older family men working in reserved occupations. . . . I suppose the total battery Home Guard complement was about 800. Some of the projectors were manned by Regulars. The senior Home Guard officer was a captain. He and his Home Guard staff controlled the operational centre at night. In short, the battery was primarily a Home Guard operational unit, although we wore the cap-badge of the County Regiment.

'An ATS Kitchen provided us with an excellent evening meal before we marched off to billets, which were large, off-site, requisitioned houses stripped bare but for bunks. We slept fully dressed except for boots, and returned at the double for an early breakfast before being dismissed.

'When we were "summoned by bells" in the night it was "boots on" and a frantic hobnail race down the road. A sergeant on the gate allocated a projector to every pair who passed him. The first one to reach it grabbed No. 1 position, which was the safer and less-demanding of the two. . . . In the pitch dark you never knew who your partner might be with a finger on the button. Loading was the responsibility of the No. 2. The No. 1 received orders [for when to fire] via his earphones. The orders were passed on from the Battery Command Centre.'

Peter Harding, who was a young engineering apprentice employed by Rolls Royce, served with the Home Guard on a gun site on the outskirts of Derby.

A Southern Railway Home Guard Anti-Aircraft Battery at Exmouth Junction Depot in Devon. (IWM)

'When the battery got the order to fire, it could put 128 rockets (each containing 56lbs of explosive) in the air together, to produce a "box" of exploding rockets at whatever altitude and bearing was given. Of course, the noise of these rockets going up was horrendous. . . .

'Occasionally, some Home Guards would go to the east coast for a weekend to relieve the regular anti-aircraft units who were in action there most nights, and I went to a battery at Sutton-on-Sea [near Mablethorpe] several times. You could almost guarantee that you would be in action at some point during the night. On the last occasion I was there a dreadful explosion occurred, and I thought the battery had received a direct hit from an enemy bomb. Later, however, I learned that one of the projectors had blown up killing all its crew. . . .'

Richard Ewing was a member of the 71st County of London 'D Troop' Heavy Anti-Aircraft Battery at Petts Wood in Kent. 'The things I remember most about being on the guns when they were in full action are the noise, the flashes from the guns lighting up the surrounding countryside like lightning, the yellowish smoke and the clanging of the empty shell cases hitting the concrete base of each gun. If you were the person who had drawn the "short straw" and your team had got a "dud", then after leaving the offending shell for thirty minutes or so you had to carry it across the gun site to the ammunition dump, in the full knowledge that at any time a large vibration could set it off. These "duds" would be blown up the following morning.'

Tales of discord between members of the Home Guard and the Regular Army crop up occasionally, but whatever may be the truth or otherwise of these stories the two

Practical training being given to men of the 2nd Southern Railway (25th Sussex) Battalion Home Guard on anti-aircraft guns positioned along the south coast.

Members of the 71st County of London Anti-Aircraft Battery's 'D' Troop at Petts Wood in Kent, 1944.

forces certainly worked together harmoniously on anti-aircraft sites, with the part-time amateurs and the full-time soldiers operating as closely-knit teams. Fred Cox was based on a gun site at Hillingdon, Middlesex. 'I must admit that the regular soldiers were very friendly. In fact, one evening the Battery Captain stood at the rear of the firing pit without me noticing. When we had finished our drill he congratulated me on the efficiency of the Home Guard team, and said that he wished his own Regulars had been able to watch it as it was so enthusiastically carried out.'

Edward Smith recalls that his Home Guard comrades at the anti-aircraft battery on Wanstead Flats – and indeed those who served alongside members of the Regular Army on gun sites everywhere – prided themselves on belonging to the only branch of the Home Guard which saw direct action against the enemy during the war. 'We had a wonderful spirit of camaraderie, even though we had to perform these spells of all-night duty in addition to going about our daily work. True, we were stood down for a few hours during the night but we certainly didn't get much rest, and to have to go to work the following morning meant that you were often very tired indeed.'

CHAPTER 7
Dad's Diverse Army

The Home Guard was nothing if not resourceful and imaginative, with dogs, pigeons, boats, horses, bicycles and even roller-skates playing their part in some of its more eccentric manifestations. In one sense these 'fancy' units, as one writer has described them, were evidence of the Home Guard's strength; further living proof of the force's ability to improvise and adapt to unusual circumstances as the need arose and, as always, set against a backdrop of inadequate resources from official channels. Seen in a different light, however, they could also be cited to reinforce the impression that has long – but I think unfairly – hovered around the Home Guard: that it was somehow slightly comic, quaint and even absurd. After all, civilians must have wondered at the time – when encountering Harry Lee's 'despatch racers' roller-skating platoon careering through the streets of London at speeds, it was estimated, of up to forty miles an hour, or chancing upon the 'Fast Cycle platoon' dashing through the lanes of Gloucestershire – what possible relevance these wholly well-intentioned groups bore to the rigours of the 'real' war that faced the population at large every day. Frank Bryant, who as a member of the War Office's clerical staff had been evacuated from London to Cheltenham, was a member of the Home Guard's 'Fast Cycle platoon'. 'A large number of us needed bicycles to get to and from work, and eventually someone thought it would be a good idea to have a Home Guard cycle platoon. About a dozen of us volunteered, as we thought that gentle cycle rides would be preferable to the usual route marches. But then we found ourselves under training by a Coldstream Guards captain, who rode not a bicycle but a motorcycle! He had the good sense to lead us from the front, although we had an almost impossible job to keep up with him. We mostly raced along the local narrow country roads and lanes, with orders frequently being barked at us to "get yourselves and your bikes over that fence, or hedge, or across that ploughed field." Our reply to the effect that we couldn't ride our bikes across the ploughed field was quickly answered by "Well, you'll have to carry them, won't you?"

'I don't remember at what stage we realised our purpose in life. It was, of course, to get to the scene of any German parachute drop in the area as quickly as possible; to fire a few rounds to slow down the enemy for the five minutes or so that he would need to register the size and scale of the opposition, thus allowing the Regular Army an extra five minutes to organise themselves into action. We were, it goes without saying, expendable.'

Dogs were employed by the Home Guard in some parts of the country and used to accompany men when out on patrol. In the main they were trained to

Britain's roller-skating champion, Harry Lee, was drafted in to train members of the Home Guard as 'despatch racers', using roller-skates to get around the capital's streets rather than more conventional means of transport. (IWM)

Members of the 'Fast Cycle Platoon', Cheltenham, Gloucestershire, 1941.

'Nell', one of the Alsatians selected for Home Guard work in north-west England, is seen here taking her proficiency test. After disarming the 'enemy', she has retrieved his gun and is taking it back to her Home Guard master. (IWM)

disarm the enemy, and the most popular breeds for this type of work were Alsatians and Mastiffs.

More unusually, perhaps, pigeons were used by some Home Guard units as message carriers. It may on the face of it seem a rather unreliable alternative to the more conventional means of transmitting information (particularly in wartime when national security was of paramount importance), but there was a case to be argued in the birds' favour. During an invasion, for example, a winged messenger might well have been more successful than a motorcycle despatch rider in reaching its intended destination without hindrance. Messages were written on extra thin paper that was then rolled into a tube and clipped to the pigeon's leg.

During an exercise held in September 1940, some members of the 6th Battalion Monmouthshire Home Guard set a pigeon and a motor-cycle despatch rider against each other in direct competition over a pre-arranged course. 'Times of departure and arrival were to be carefully checked for future reference and guidance,' explained the subsequent official report of the proceedings. 'At the "off" the betting was evens, but odds on the pigeon shortened considerably when it was discovered by the touts that the pigeon had been given a secret trial on the previous Sunday, and an excellent time recorded. Both starters were surrounded in the paddock by their respective admirers, the messages written, handed over and attached respectively. . . . The pigeon proved an easy winner. The motor-cycle despatch rider lost an important accessory from his bike en route, and was of the decided opinion that,

A Home Guard carrier pigeon being sent off with a message, Gloucestershire, 1942. (IWM)

during the inspection in the paddock prior to the start, someone interested in the pigeon service must have been allowed much too near his machine!'

Needless to say, the Home Guard pigeons were officially recognised and regulated, as this extract from the War Office's 'Regulations for the Home Guard, 1942' confirms. '. . . Arrangements for the operation of all pigeon services which are required for Home Guard communications will be made by Chief Signal Officers, who will issue standard pigeon equipment and allocate suitable Pigeon Supply Officers (PSOs) and National Pigeon Service (NPS) lofts for their use where available. . . . Pigeon food required for birds held on service for over 48 hours will be provided by commands who will indent though the usual channels. . . .' In addition, a specially designed Army Form (No. G988) had to be filled in whenever birds were despatched, and all communications sent on the wing were transcribed on to what was officially called a Pigeon Message Form.

Mounted units of the Home Guard were established almost – although not quite – exclusively in the country's wilder and more remote areas, including Exmoor and Dartmoor, the North Yorkshire Moors, the hills of North Wales and parts of the Cumberland and Westmorland fells. Mostly comprising members drawn from the local farming and hunting fraternities, men who were closely acquainted with every square inch of their terrain, these units were of inestimable value in their ability to comb areas of the country that would have been

A detachment of Home Guard formed up near Middle Tor, Chagford, before going to their various posts on Dartmoor, 1940. (IWM)

inaccessible to the motor car and too vast to cover on foot. Horses, therefore, were the ideal solution for patrolling these extensive moorland and upland regions which, because of the privacy they afforded, were so vulnerable to potential enemy parachute landings. Given the tendency for impenetrable mists to sweep over the moors and fells, one wonders how often the Home Guard and enemy parachutists would actually have found one another!.

Evelyn Radley, now of Barnstaple, recalls how her husband became a member of the Mounted Home Guard in 1940 when he farmed on the western edge of Exmoor. 'Their duties in those early days were to ride out at daybreak and patrol a particular area of the moors for two hours or so working in pairs. At first the men were armed only with hunting crops, although later they were issued with rifles. . . . They each went out on average two mornings a week, although the troop also met on Sunday afternoons for training in how to correctly mount and dismount their horses! On these occasions they also practised the art of concealing themselves and their horses in whatever hiding places were available. My husband told of how one member remarked on being spotted, "Ah well, I shall just have to find a bigger quarry – or get a smaller horse."'

Mounted units of the Home Guard could also be found on the South Downs, where one group patrolled under the banner of the optimistically-named 'Lewes Cossacks'. More unusual, though, suburban Maidenhead also boasted a platoon

A veteran of the First World War gives a member of the North Yorkshire Moors Mounted Home Guard a few tips on shooting from the saddle, 1940. (IWM)

of Home Guards on horseback. Comprising members of the local Garth Hunt, farmers and jockeys, it was hoped that this mounted Berkshire unit would prove to be of valuable service should local roads become sufficiently damaged in the course of enemy action as to prevent the flow of more conventional traffic.

Battalion Commanders were required to seek special permission from the War Office before they could establish a mounted patrol, and among the conditions governing the existence of these so-called 'sub units' (again laid down in 'Regulations for the Home Guard, 1942'), were that '. . . the horses will be provided

A mounted Home Guard unit on patrol in South Wales.

by the units themselves. The patrol leader will ensure that only sound horses, fit for the duties they are to perform, are used. . . . On account of the extra expense incurred by owners in keeping horses fit for Home Guard duties, an allowance of 15/- a month is admissable for each authorised horse and its equipment. . . . In addition to the normal civilian ration of forage, "Horse-feed" ration coupons to permit purchase of a maximum quantity of 1½ cwt of forage a month for the period 1 April–30 September and 2 cwt of forage a month for the period 1 October– 31 March are authorised for each horse used on approved patrols. . . .'

Under these War Office 'Regulations', the men who served in mounted patrols were also permitted a variation in the standard Home Guard uniform. 'An issue of one pair of pantaloons, Bedford cord, and one pair of puttees, ordinary, is authorised . . . in replacement of trousers, battledress and anklets. On receipt of the pantaloons and puttees, the trousers and anklets already issued will be withdrawn. . . .' Compensation for the loss of, or any damage sustained by, a horse through enemy action while out on Home Guard duties was governed by the War Damage Act.

Away from dry land, the Home Guard soon got to grips with patrolling and guarding some of the country's rivers, lakes and inland waterways. One of the earliest – and perhaps best organised – of these quasi-nautical outfits was the Upper Thames Patrol (UTP). Within only a few days of Eden's call for the formation of a civilian army to defend the Home Front, Sir Ralph Glyn, the Tory Member of Parliament for Abingdon, requested permission from the War Minister to set up a waterborne unit of the LDV along the upper reaches of the Thames. Its purpose was to patrol the river and to keep watch over bridges, locks, weirs and riverside pumping stations, all of which were deemed to be at risk from enemy action. Various units were established to protect that part of the Thames which flows between

An Upper Thames Patrol launch with crew on duty, July 1940. (IWM)

Lechlade in Gloucestershire and Teddington in Middlesex (a distance of over 120 miles); each patrol being divided into stretches of sixteen miles and each presided over by a 'stretch-commander'. Men with experience of handling boats and a knowledge of the river were particularly welcome in the UTP and, as a result, many an old sailor was given the opportunity to revive his nautical skills.

James White was a member of the UTP's Stretch B1 based at Reading. 'When first formed the UTP came under the control of the Royal Navy. The uniform consisted of army battledress, seaman's blue roll-neck jersey, blue peaked cap, sea-boot socks and Wellington boots. . . . We were trained in the handling of boats, tying and splicing of rope knots, semaphore signalling with flags and general rivercraft. Our boats consisted of launches and cabin-cruisers commandeered from private owners and painted battleship grey. In addition to three parade and training evenings per week, our duties were to patrol the stretch of river from Reading Lock to Mapledurham. Also, we had rifle training on Sunday mornings and attended evening lectures on first-aid, map-reading and unarmed combat. . . .'

Michael Brooks was a senior pupil at Radley College, Abingdon, and recalls that '. . . the Radley Unit of the UTP was responsible for patrolling the Thames from Sandford Lock down to the main line railway bridge above Abingdon, which was thought to be a likely target for sabotage by parachutists. . . . The Radley patrol had its HQ in the College boat-house, and patrolling was carried out using the College slipper launch *Lusimus*, for which a special ration of fuel was provided. I well recall nights spent on these patrols, sleeping uncomfortably

A speedy vessel belonging to the Trent River Patrol, camouflaged and protected by a machine-gun in the stern. (IWM)

on straw palliasses in the boat-house between spells of duty, brewing up when the tea ration allowed and listening to the drone of enemy aircraft. . . .'

Further north, the Trent River Patrol sprang into action barely a month after the formation of the LDV, and mounted a dusk to dawn surveillance along the River Trent from Sawley (south of Nottingham) through to the Humber estuary. The TRP developed into a highly efficient waterborne organisation with over 100 miles of river to protect; although Len Murray, who served in a patrol based at a rowing club near Trent Bridge, recalls one incident which could have had tragic results but fortunately ended without injury. The sergeant of the patrol had gone ashore to make contact with a land-based Home Guard unit further downstream, while his crew – except for a sentry posted on guard duty – rested below deck. 'It was still quite dark when the sergeant returned, and stepped carefully on deck from the landing-stage. . . . His first action should have been to clear the magazine of his rifle but alas he failed to do so. After tiptoeing across the deck to avoid waking the sleeping warriors below, he sat on the step leading down to the saloon, and as he leaned forward to put his weapon down there was a tremendous bang from the obviously cocked rifle. The sleeping figures, blankets and all, were halfway through the door in a split second heading for safety, and their remarks made the air blue. There were no casualties, but as the boat cast off and prepared to proceed upriver the obvious question gradually dawned. Where had the round made its exit? The bilge boards were hurriedly pulled up to reveal a slowly

A world away from the leafier reaches of the Upper Thames, members of the Port of London Authority Home Guard are pictured here on duty in the West India Docks in the East End. (IWM)

growing depth of water in the bilge!'

Elsewhere, waterborne units of the Home Guard patrolled the canal system that wound its way through the heart of industrial Birmingham; while others mounted watch over the Norfolk Broads, where patrols kept a keen look-out not only for descending parachutists but also for enemy seaplanes that might seize the opportunity of landing on these larger expanses of water.

In the Lake District, members of the waterborne section of the 9th Westmorland Battalion Home Guard patrolled Windermere. The unit, which comprised two groups (one based in the town of Windermere itself and the other at nearby Bowness), covered all 10½ miles of the lake from Waterhead in the north to Lakeside in the south. A decade earlier, the children's novelist Arthur Ransome had set his classic *Swallows and Amazons* – a tale of sailing, fishing and piracy in the school holidays – on an amalgam of Coniston Water and Windermere. Now the lake was the real-life setting for activities of an altogether more sombre kind. The hill country bounding the lake, and the wooded slopes of the Furness Fells on its western shores south of Esthwaite Water, would have been ideal terrain for clandestine enemy parachute drops. A keen watch also had to be kept for any German waterborne landings on what is, after all, the region's largest lake.

It would be all-too easy to decry the notion of Home Guards afloat or on horseback, or even on bicycles and roller-skates, as some of the force's critics have done over the years. But perhaps it would be more appropriate to view these aspects of Britain's civilian army as earlier manifestations of the concept so lovingly espoused by generations of presenters on that most famous of all children's television programmes, *Blue Peter*; who, in demonstrating how to build a doll's house or construct a nesting-box using the most basic of materials, showed that it was entirely possible to create something useful, functional and worthwhile by employing the minimum of resources.

CHAPTER 8
Dad's Daughter's Army

When Anthony Eden made his historic broadcast to a hushed and expectant nation on the evening of 14 May 1940, he specifically requested that men should offer themselves for enrolment in the Local Defence Volunteers. '. . . We want large numbers of men,' he said, 'to come forward now and offer their services. . . .' No mention was made of women playing a part in Britain's new civilian army; in fact, they were entirely excluded from the Secretary of State's appeal. It wasn't – hopefully – a case of ignorance or blind sexism on the War Office's part, but more likely a recognition of the fact that women in the war already had a considerable burden to bear, not to mention a number of existing avenues through which they could channel their zeal for voluntary war work and thus make a positive contribution to daily life on the Home Front.

For many women during the war, of course, the responsibilities of keeping a home going and bringing up a family were made even more demanding than usual in the absence of husbands who were abroad serving with the Regular Forces, and in the prevailing climate of danger and austerity. Despite these difficulties, however, many women all over the country were already making their contribution to the war effort; anything from driving ambulances and fire engines to working in munitions factories and other industries. Many served with the Civil Defence or joined the Auxiliary Armed Forces. With the prospect of war growing ever more real, the Women's Voluntary Service (WVS) had been formed in 1938, and its thousands of members provided a wide range of support for the civilian population, Civil Defence and other services throughout the course of the hostilities. The manufacturing firm Hoover was prompt to issue a poster bearing its 'Salute to the Women of England' (although one wonders what women from other parts of the British Isles thought of their exclusion from this tribute). '. . . Women who have left their homes and friends and familiar surroundings to don a uniform and take any job they can do – from ferrying a four-engine bomber to peeling potatoes! Women who have worked on at their factory benches, unperturbed by the siren screaming. And, too, the women who are doing a double job in this war; who, day after day, run their homes and yet do war work as well; who cope with shopping queues and cooking and cleaning, yet turn up for their shift at the factory smiling. . . .'

Probably the most famous women's organisation to spring up during the Second World War, and one that still evokes waves of nostalgia whenever it is mentioned, was the Women's Land Army. (Although not as long-lived as *Dad's Army*, the WLA spawned its own TV sitcom *Backs to the Land* during the 1970s, and was also the subject of a recent successful feature film, *The Land Girls*, based on Angela Huth's 1994 novel of the same name). Originally formed in 1917, the Women's Land Army was resurrected on a far larger scale during the Second World War and, by the summer of 1943, nearly 77,000 Land Girls were working on farms up and down the country. As S.P. MacKenzie comments in his book *The Home Guard* (1996), it is likely the War Office reasoned that, were women to be admitted to the Home Guard, then the number available to serve in these other already established and vital occupations and organisations might fall as a result.

Women up to the age of forty were classed as either 'mobile' or 'immobile', depending on their family circumstances – a 'mobile' woman was someone with no domestic ties, who could be sent to do essential war work in any part of the country where she was needed – but, as Raynes Minns observed in *Bombers & Mash* (1980), her comprehensive account of life on the 'domestic front' during the Second World War, there was in fact a great deal of pressure placed on all women to play their full part in the war effort, as this extract from a BBC broadcast dating from mid-1941 confirms: 'Today we are calling all women. Every woman in the country is needed to pull her weight to the utmost; to consider carefully where her services would help most and then let nothing stand in the way of rendering such services. . . . It is no longer a question of what is the most comfortable arrangement for each family. We are fighting for our lives, for our freedom and future. We are all in it together, and what is already being done by other women you can do. . . .'

Raynes Minns records that, by June 1943, 9 out of 10 single women and 8 out of 10 married women aged between 18 and 40 were either in the Forces or working in industry; and that the remainder were caring either for the young or old or billeters, doing part-time work and out-work at home. It is a fascinating statistic, drawn from the middle of the year that women were eventually – but somewhat half-heartedly – admitted into the Home Guard as Auxiliaries. They were not permitted to carry weapons, and an identity badge or armlet was all that served as a uniform. In the event, fewer women than had been expected took advantage of this new opportunity, although the government's statistics regarding female enrolment would not have taken account of the large – but necessarily unquantified – number of women who were already acting unofficially as volunteers with Home Guard units throughout the land, and who had been serving in that capacity ever since the force had come into existence.

As if anticipating events of the following year, the Commanding Officer of the 34th Warwickshire (Birmingham) Battalion Home Guard wrote in October 1942 that his Battalion '. . . was the first to realise the assistance which could be forthcoming from women, and has a unit known as the Women's Auxiliary 34th Battalion, which staffs Signals Office, Intelligence Office and provides the necessary clerical and other assistance.'

The experiences of the eighty-four ladies who served as Auxiliaries with the 13th North Staffordshire (Cannock) Battalion Home Guard are probably fairly

A young lady at the wheel of an Upper Thames Patrol launch in July 1940, three years before women were officially admitted to the Home Guard as Auxiliaries. (IWM)

typical. The Battalion's official historian records that they '. . . were recruited for such jobs as telephonists, typists, clerks, car drivers and cooks. It seems fitting that the communication exercises were all titled with feminine names, for the clerks, telephonists and typists proved their worth in the Signals and Intelligence Offices during these exercises.

'The truth of Napoleon's maxim that "an army marches on its stomach" points to the importance, militarily, of the Home Guard ladies recruited to act as cooks. During social evenings . . . the cooks managed to get some training by preparing and serving refreshments. All guests at these functions were highly delighted with the foretaste of what food they might expect if called upon to do active service.'

Joan Tickner, who served as a Woman Home Guard Auxiliary in Middlesex, can vouch from personal experience for the faith placed in Napoleon's words by some members of the force. 'We ladies actually joined the Home Guard on their weekly exercises, learning such things as how to use a Tommy gun, Morse Code etc., and also self-defence. . . . One lovely summer's evening we were on an exercise at a large country house surrounded by extensive grounds at Ealing. After being issued with my password for the night, the moment came when I had to present myself to the officer-in-charge and receive my instructions. Imagine

Two ladies, Miss Becky Robbins and Mrs Stone, who served as Women Auxiliaries with the Southern Railway Home Guard in Surrey.

my disappointment when I was told, in all seriousness, that I had been allocated to shell the peas for the Officers' meal that evening! Later, after midnight, I was allowed three hours' sleep on bare boards in a bare attic room. Luckly I had brought my own blanket and pillow.'

Phyllis Woodham was a wartime employee of the Hearts of Oak Benefit Society, which had been evacuated from London's Euston Road to the remote and moated Herstmonceux Castle in East Sussex. The castle was also home to 'C' Company of the 20th Sussex (Hailsham) Battalion Home Guard. Miss Woodham recalls that she was asked '. . . together with seven other girls to volunteer to cook for the Home Guard, who were going on a weekend exercise. With absolutely no idea of what we were letting ourselves in for we arrived at the local vicarage, which had been requisitioned by the Army as the headquarters for the Sussex Regiment which had recently returned from service overseas. I shall never forget the looks on the soldiers' faces when eight girls attired in summer dresses and sporting LDV armbands and frilly aprons stepped off a lorry. However, they did appreciate what we had taken on and proceeded to show us how to make gallons of tea and to peel hundreds of potatoes. With the help of the Army we managed to feed the Home Guard and it was decided to make us official members of the force. We were trained in Intelligence and Signalling and became "runners" on later exercises.'

Lois Baker of Croydon recalls that '. . . as a young clerk in the Air Ministry . . . I was in a reserved occupation as also were the Heads of our Departments, who were mostly men in their 40s. The men became the Officers and other ranks of the Air Ministry Battalion of the Home Guard. We girls had already volunteered

Time to say goodbye, as a group of Home Guard Women Auxiliaries gather in King's Lynn for their Stand Down ceremony at the end of 1944.

for fire-watching and first aid duties but were longing for the glamour of a uniform, and so we asked if we too could join the Home Guard. . . . [Eventually] the Air Ministry Auxiliary Section of the Home Guard was formed to provide back-up for the men.

'The only uniform [that members of this particular unit of] "Dad's Daughter's Army" were allowed was a navy blue boiler suit, navy "fore and aft" cap, service tin hat and respirator. . . . We paraded weekly and some were detailed to be cooks, some to be signallers. I was one of the latter, to be taught Morse Code (or, rather, revise it as I had been a Girl Guide).

'I wonder how much support we could have given in an emergency? . . . Fortunately this was never put to the test, but for us it was a wonderful morale booster.'

Ann Eggar of Minehead 'thoroughly enjoyed' her time with the Home Guard during which, she recalls, 'I was lucky enough to be allowed to attend a small-arms course for the Home Guard run by members of the Canadian Army, during which I was taught to handle everything from revolvers to rifles and Sten guns, including how to throw grenades. Then a British Army officer visited the course to see how the training was progressing, and he was

**20th Sussex (HAILSHAM) Battalion
Home Guard.**

Telephone :- Hailsham 213/4

H.Q. New Drill Hall,
Hailsham.

December 1944

        Now that the Home Guard has received its
"Stand Down" orders our happy association with
our Home Guard Auxiliaries comes to an end.

        We should like, however, to express our
very sincere thanks and appreciation of the willing
and useful work you have performed especially in
connection with the Intelligence and Signalling
Sections: we know that your duties would have
been efficiently carried out, if the need had arisen.

        We thought that you would like to have the
enclosed photograph of our C.O's portrait, which he
has kindly autographed, and hope that it will remind
you of many happy hours whilst serving with the
20th Sx Bn Home Guard.

Harold R H Morgan

Captain
I.O. 20th Sx(Hailsham)Bn HG

G C Procter

Lieut.
Sigs Offr 20th Sx(Hailsham)Bn HG

*A 'thank you' letter sent to Home Guard Woman Auxiliary
Phyllis Woodham at Stand Down from her Battalion
Commander.*

I have received The King's command
to express His Majesty's appreciation
of the loyal service given voluntarily
to her country in a time of grievous danger
by *Miss Phyllis Woodham*

as a Woman Home Guard Auxiliary.

The War Office,
London.

Secretary of State
for War

*Phyllis Woodham's personal message of thanks from the King
at Stand Down.*

immediately horrified by my presence. He talked about the Geneva Convention forbidding women to be armed, and demanded my absence from any future training sessions.'

Pamela Housden was attached to an anti-aircraft rocket battery on Merseyside where she served as a full-time Battery Secretary, even earning a small salary into the bargain. Her job '. . . consisted of typing correspondence, making out Platoon lists and instructions, checking attendance records, etc.' Being based on Merseyside, she witnessed some dramatic and frightening episodes, not least the occasion when a fatally damaged American Flying Fortress crash-landed in the garden outside her makeshift office with the loss of all the crew on board. Nevertheless, she recalls being '. . . very sad at Stand Down. It had been an amazing period in everyone's lives and one made good friends. Although it was exhausting work on top of the "day job", the Unit became a cherished club, much missed but remembered with pride and affection. Churchill's psychology had been very sound in his support of the Home Guard. It was so much more fulfilling to be able to do something with other people, rather than to wait around helplessly taking everything that was flung at us.'

Although women were not given an opportunity to participate in Britain's civilian army to the same degree as their male counterparts, the contribution they made to the efficiency and smooth running of the force in a supporting but vital role was of inestimable value, and was officially recognised after Stand Down when every Woman Home Guard Auxiliary received a personal message of thanks from the King via the War Office, for '. . . loyal service given voluntarily to her country in a time of grievous danger. . . .'

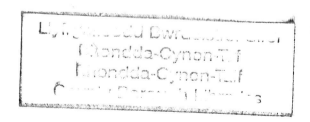

CHAPTER 9

Dad's 'Secret Army'

It has been described as one of the war's best-kept and most enduring secrets. Indeed, only over the course of the past few decades, as details of the organisation have appeared in print, have some members of Britain's Auxiliary Units begun to speak openly about the existence of this élite guerrilla force which was established in the coastal counties of Britain.

To describe these Auxiliary Units as the Home Guard's 'Secret Army', a title that has been freely applied to them over the years not only in press reports and radio and television documentaries but also by many former members themselves, is actually to misrepresent their position. Without a doubt, hand picked members of the Home Guard were invited to join this underground – literally so in many cases, as will be seen – movement. However, it would be more accurate to say that the Auxiliary Units capitalised on the existence of the Home Guard, using it as a highly effective smokescreen for their own secret activities, and that as time went on their ranks comprised many men – and women too – who had no connection whatsoever with the Home Guard. Nevertheless, the joint histories of the Home Guard and the Auxiliary Units are so closely intertwined in the public imagination that an account of this so-called 'British Resistance' movement has a valid place here.

A letter sent to Prime Minister Churchill from the offices of the War Cabinet at the beginning of August 1940 explains the purpose of the Auxiliary Units (a title that was deliberately kept vague for the sake of secrecy). 'These Auxiliary Units,' it read, 'are being formed with two objectives: a) They are intended to provide, within the framework of the Home Guard organisation, small bodies of men especially selected and trained, whose role it will be to act offensively on the flanks and in the rear of any enemy troops who may obtain a foothold in this country. Their action will particularly be directed against tanks and lorries . . . ammunition dumps, small enemy posts and stragglers. Their activities will also include sniping. b) The other function of the Auxiliary Units is to provide a system of intelligence, whereby the Regular Forces in the field can be kept informed of what is happening behind enemy lines. . . .' Among other things, the letter went on to explain that each unit would usually comprise less than a dozen men, most of whom would be recruited from among the farming and game-keeping fraternity, together with others who were well acquainted with the local countryside in which they would be operating; that, in addition to the provision of weapons and explosive devices, they would be equipped with wireless and field telephone apparatus to assist with their intelligence work, and that each unit would be accommodated in specially prepared and concealed hideouts (known as 'operational bases' or OBs) where reserves of food and water, weapons and ammunition could all be safely stored for long periods if it proved to be necessary. The location of each hideout was to be – and, as it turned out in many cases, would remain for years – a matter of the greatest secrecy. 'All the activities of these Auxiliary Units,' the letter pointed out, 'are under the direct supervision of Colonel Colin Gubbins, who himself is on the GHQ Staff of Home Forces, and are planned and carried out in the closest collaboration with the military authorities in the areas concerned.'

That some confusion arose over the separate identities of the Home Guard and the Auxiliary Units is quite understandable. (In fact, the letter referred to above goes on to describe Auxiliary Units as 'this new branch of the Home Guard'). Members of the so-called 'Secret Army', whether actually serving in the Home Guard or not, were recruited into three specially formed battalions ostensibly of the Home Guard – the 201st in Scotland, the 202nd in the north of England and the 203rd in the south of England – and they were also issued with Home Guard uniforms to wear. But, as David Lampe pointed out in *The Last Ditch* (1969), his meticulously researched account of Auxiliary Units, none of these battalions (which were all attached to GHQ Home Forces) actually appeared in the Home Guard's own official records, such was the high degree of secrecy which surrounded their very existence.

It was the assumption that German forces would invade this country by sea rather than by air that led to the Auxiliary Units being placed in locations around Britain's coastline. As David Lampe explains, the first units were set up in those areas of the country considered most vulnerable to enemy invasion: Kent and Sussex, East Anglia and around the coastlines of Devon and Cornwall. 'Eventually,' Lampe continues, 'there were Auxiliary Units patrols covering an almost unbroken thirty-mile coastal belt extending from Cape Wrath in the north-west of Scotland around the country clockwise to central Wales, but North Wales and the north-west coasts of England and Scotland were left undefended because the Germans would almost certainly have ruled out these areas as landing places. No attempt was ever made by Auxiliary Units to set up an organisation in Northern Ireland.'

Appropriately, given the clandestine and essentially rural nature of the Auxiliary Units' activities, the Headquarters of this organisation was to be found not as one might expect in London, close to the seat of government, but at Coleshill House, a country mansion set in its own secluded and extensive grounds between Faringdon and Highworth to the north-east of Swindon. The seventeenth-century house ('. . . one of the most perfect houses in England', according to an old guide issued by the National Trust, who now own the land on which it stood) was designed by Inigo Jones. Sadly the property can no longer be seen as it was destroyed by a fire in the 1950s; a blaze that was apparently caused by a painter's unattended blowlamp being left turned on. Owing to Coleshill's wartime connection with the Auxiliary Units, however, it is perhaps inevitable that conspiracy theories abound concerning its untimely end.

Anyone travelling to Coleshill House, whether for training purposes or on some other Auxiliary Units business, soon discovered that it was not simply a matter of turning up on the front doorstep of this impressive mansion and announcing their arrival; there was a convoluted but highy effective security procedure to be negotiated first, one that could almost have been lifted straight from the pages of a John Buchan novel. Having been instructed to report to 'GHQ Auxiliary Units, c/o Highworth, Wilts.', visitors found themselves being received at the local post office by none other than the postmistress herself, Mrs Mabel Stranks. Another in a long and distinguished line of the war's self-effacing and unsung heroes, Mrs Stranks played a small part in the affairs of the Auxiliary Units which even today is not entirely clear, beyond the fact that she served in some way as a one-woman reception committee or 'vetting agent' for visitors and potential recruits arriving at Highworth; and acted in this capacity on behalf of the commanders of the 'Secret Army', who were lodged nearby at Coleshill House. David Lampe explains how, when visitors presented themselves at the post office in Highworth, Mrs Stranks '. . . would ask to see proof of their identity and would leave them. A few minutes later she would return and say simply 'Somebody's coming to fetch you.' After that she would go on about her business and refuse to answer any questions. Soon either a civilian car or a military vehicle with a red and white plate bearing the GHQ Home Forces identification number 490 would turn up to take the new arrivals to the headquarters.'

In June 2000, the *Western Daily Press* reported that Highworth was hoping to officially honour its former postmistress by erecting a plaque in her memory outside the old post office. The unveiling ceremony was performed in October 2001. By the time of her death in 1971, Mrs Stranks had apparently divulged few details of her highly sensitive wartime role either to friends or members of her family. However, in the same newspaper report a former member of the Auxiliary Units who had been 'vetted' by the postmistress said that had she been captured by the enemy, '. . . I think she would have been tortured, because she knew everything about the "Secret Army".'

It is impossible to emphasise enough – or exaggerate – the degree of secrecy which surrounded the existence of the Auxiliary Units. The men who made up the organisation in the field – women were also recruited, mainly to operate the Resistance wireless network – consisted of small scattered cells, each of which was to a large extent unaware of the existence or location of other similar units, even though they were all engaged in the same pursuit. Politicans, (beyond Churchill and a few other very senior figures), the military and Home Guard hierarchy were all kept firmly in the dark. It was hardly surprising that, in this 'cloak and dagger' atmosphere, the men themselves divulged nothing of this 'other' life to their wives, families and friends. Even when the Auxiliary Units handbook on sabotage techniques was issued for use by members in 1942 (it was actually distributed on a very limited basis to patrol leaders and, it is said, this was one of the few instances when anything relating to the existence or work of the 'Secret Army' was put into print), it was disguised as 'The Countryman's Diary – 1939', and bore the following announcement on its cover:

> Highworth Fertilisers
> Do their stuff unseen
> Until you see
> Results!
> With the compliments of
> Highworth & Co.
> You will find the name Highworth
> Wherever quick results
> Are required.

Although this would have seemed like a straightforward advertisement to the layman, members of the Auxiliary Units would have been able to read between the lines with ease.

When, in 1994, a commemorative luncheon was held at the Church Hall, Coleshill, for surviving members of the Auxiliary Units, to mark the fiftieth anniversary of the 'Secret Army's' disbandment, 'Highworth Fertilisers do their stuff unseen' was written across the official invitation.

Frederick Simpson was recruited as a member of the Auxiliary Units on the Isle of Purbeck in Dorset, and he has written a vivid account of his time spent with the 'Secret Army'. Initially, he had enrolled as a member of his local Home Guard, serving as a despatch rider and using his own motorbike, '. . . but I soon became bored with it, and when a call came for volunteers for a dangerous job I, together with three others, stepped forward and, with two or three from a neighbouring village, we were taken out of the Home Guard and formed into a patrol of seven men – all poachers, gamekeepers, farm or country men. We were given uniforms and denim overalls, and a shoulder tape with the words "Auxiliary Regiment" with a patch below numbered "203". All square bashing stopped and, after signing the Official Secrets Act, we became guerrillas.

'We were then told what was expected of us. We were to hide when the Germans invaded and come up behind their lines to play "merry hell" with them. This involved blowing up petrol dumps, laying mines and booby traps across roads and paths, cutting railway lines, blowing down trees across roads. . . . To do this we first of all had to dig an underground hideout. Our first one in dense forest very quickly collapsed, but we dug another one. I made some hurdles from hazel backed with bracken as it was very sandy soil. Five of us spent two days and nights in this one to test the air, and we found it foul. We cooked meals on a primus stove – just boiled potatoes and eggs mainly, and nothing fried because the smell of frying could be detected on the surface some way away. . . . [Later], it was decided to do things properly and troops from the Pioneer Corps were sent in to build us a bunker. . . . [It] consisted of two rooms built of concrete blocks and curved steel sheets. The first room was for living and storage and the second, connected by a small passage set at an angle so that any grenade or other explosion would not affect both rooms, was for sleeping. Here we had naval hammocks erected star fashion . . . and at one end of this sleeping area we had a bolt hole to the surface, the main entrance being via a secret trap door on which was planted grass, ferns and small trees for camouflage. To enter from outside, one had to look for a cotton

The underground hideout situated on the Isle of Purbeck in Dorset where Frederick Simpson spent many hours as a member of Britain's 'Secret Army'. Like many others around the country, this operational base was blown up by the Royal Engineers once its purpose had come to an end.

reel hidden in a clump of bushes. On pulling this a steel wire raised the trap door just a little so that it could then be swivelled round on its support exposing a shaft with a ladder. This entrance to the first room was still blocked by a heavy wooden door on rollers which could only be opened from the inside. . . . This would have given us a chance to escape through the bolt hole if beseiged. . . .

'The stores to be kept were ammunition, explosives, a certain amount of food and a gallon of rum in a stone jar. At the end of the war all these were collected by the Ordnance Corps, but one of the patrols had drilled a hole in the bottom of their jar and drunk the rum. [Owing to the extreme circumstances in which members of the Auxiliary Units would have gone into action, the issue of rum was intended strictly for emergency use only !]. They then filled up the hole with cement but, like fools, we allowed our rum to be returned. . . .

'The first personal weapon issued to me was a Stanley kitchen knife, and I attended a course on how to apprehend the enemy using the knife. Later on we were given Browning automatics, Colt revolvers (later changed to Smith & Wessons), SAS-type daggers [no doubt the Fairbairn Commando dagger, which was issued to everyone in Auxiliary Units], Thompson sub-machine guns, .303 rifles (later changed to Sten guns) and .22 sniper rifles with telescopic sights and a silencer. These were some of our weapons, but the "tools" for the job were mainly explosives, [including] gelignite, blasting gelatine, phosphorous grenades, etc. . . .

'We were sent to various army training depots: one locally at Duntish Court and another at Swindon [probably Coleshill House]. . . . Nobody, not even our parents, knew what we were doing and we kept our silence. . . . We had no disbandment parade, as did the Home Guard, at the end of the war; we just gave up our supplies, though we kept our greatcoats and two pairs of boots. . . . Later came a letter of thanks from the War Office, and after one reunion dinner we ceased to be. The Royal Engineers blew up our bunker. . . .

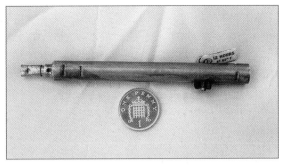

An L-delay, or Lead Delay. As its name suggests, this was a delay mechanism for explosive charges used by members of Auxiliary Units. Stewart Angell, who supplied this photograph, explains that the time it took to set the charge off was dictated by the thickness of lead wire used internally. The L-Delay seen here was kept by Frank Dean, leader of the Rodmell Patrol in Sussex. It is now housed in the British Resistance Museum at Parham, Suffolk.

'One thing which we were proud of was being chosen on D-Day to guard one of the very few radar and wireless stations working at that time, which was in the Purbeck Hills and buried underground. . . . Our instructions were to meet at Wareham . . . [and] we were picked up in army lorries and taken to the hills above Swanage, under both canvas and army orders.'

Here is a brief extract relating to that occasion, taken from Mr Simpson's diary of events in June 1944:

2.30 meet at Wareham, army lorries to Knitson Farm
4.30 transferred to hilltop to guard installations, tents erected, camouflage nets on everything. RAF Regiment and guard dogs on all day, Auxiliary Units at night. Tea at 5.30.
Next morning assembling equipment, laying tripwires and booby traps on all approach paths and gaps, leaving pins in.
11 p.m. Mounted guard after pulling out all safety pins. 3 sentry posts, triangular setting, arms: two Tommy guns, one Sten, all loaded. Changed posts clockwise every hour – crawling. Warned to expect paratroops or sea-transported saboteurs. Challenge anyone walking, shoot to kill any person crawling, fire at any suspicious movement.
Cold lying on ground, no cover, high wind, one walking challenge, else OK. Planes all night, flares over sea and French coast. Heavy gunfire or bombs over channel. Two hospital ships coming back all lit up with red cross. Off duty at 2 a.m., second guard arrives. . . .'

'I don't know what would have happened if the Germans had invaded,' reflects Mr Simpson. 'The worst of it was knowing that our families, if not dead, would have been in enemy hands and liable to be shot if we started anything. . . . To know

This hideout, photographed by Stewart Angell in 1994, belonged to the Staplefield Patrol based in Foxashes Wood west of Haywards Heath in Sussex. Bunk beds can be seen on the right and the open door leads to an entrance shaft.

that we would not last long after our first attack did not bother us; I am sure we would have fulfilled our purpose, which was to hinder the enemy as far as we could, and though we had no cyanide capsules we had at no time to let ourselves be captured, alive or injured, thereby being tortured to reveal our base or companions. Knowing now the methods used by the German forces, I can see what decisions we as a unit, and for that matter the whole structure of Auxiliary Units, would have to make. The joke was "keep the last bullet for yourself"! . . . But, nevertheless, if we could keep a small section or even a battalion of the enemy occupied for a time, they would not be available to face our main defence. . . .'

The siting and construction of suitable hideouts called for reserves of much ingenuity around the country. David Lampe records how long abandoned tin mines in Cornwall and disused coal mines in Wales and the north-east of England were found to be highly suitable for the Auxiliary Units' purpose, as were ancient Pictish dwellings in the north of Scotland and – at the other end of Britain – tunnels and underground rooms that had been excavated in the chalk on the Isle of Thanet when smuggling was rife in that area.

Ed Maltby served with the Auxiliary Units around the village of Bubwith in the former East Riding of Yorkshire, but his patrol was unable to construct a suitable hideout below ground, although the men devised a highly ingenious alternative. 'It was impossible to go underground due to the high water-table. Our

THE
BRITISH
RESISTANCE
ORGANISATION
1940 - 1944

INSIGNIA OF
AUXILIARY UNITS
BATTALIONS
201 SCOTLAND
202 NORTH OF THAMES
203 SOUTH OF THAMES

GHQ HOME FORCES
SHOULDER BADGE
OF HQ STAFF
AND
AUXILIARY UNITS
SIGNALS

The little-known – and rarely seen – insignia of Britain's Auxiliary Units.

first hideout was established in a stable on a nearby farm. It was a long stable and a wall was constructed across the far end from the door, making the interior of the building seem shorter than it actually was. The entrance was a section of wall which sprang back when pressed in the right place, but it was found that anyone entering the stable could hear voices in the hideout and so we had to abandon it and start again.

'There was an old windmill and miller's house lying between two of our villages and the house was long uninhabited. A small Nissen hut was constructed in this house and passages built as entries. These passages were about three feet high and the same width. The house was then collapsed on to the hideout and a dummy bomb crater made at the side. Entry was obtained by crawling under the ruin and again pushing a certain section of the wall to gain admittance. There was an emergency exit at the other end of the hideout which led into a grassy field where, by sliding back two bolts from inside the tunnel, a trap door would swing down. From outside, the door appeared to be just a part of the grass covering the field.'

Only the young and the very fit were recruited and trained for service in the patrols of the Auxiliary Units, and the average age of members was estimated at under thirty years. The task for which they were being prepared, to spring into action behind enemy lines in the event of an invasion, was a ruthless one. The code by which these men would have been forced to live in order to preserve the secrecy of their existence was no less brutal. F.D. Chisholm, who served with a patrol in North Yorkshire, explains: 'We had to take no prisoners nor be taken prisoner, and the sad thing was that if one of our number were wounded in action and unable to escape or walk, we would have had to kill him by using a length of wire that we each carried. We could not afford to leave anybody behind, and we had to be cruel to be kind. The Germans would have tortured him and put him to death anyway. Not even my own mother knew what I was doing, neither did my brothers and sisters nor my girl friend who I later married. I knew that there were other young men doing the same thing as myself, but for safety's sake we were never given any information. . . .'

The Auxiliary Units were stood down at the same time as the Home Guard. All members received a letter dated 30 November 1944, signed by their Commander at that time, Colonel Frank Douglas, informing them that their services were no longer required. 'I realise what joining the Auxiliary Units has meant to you', it read. '. . . You were invited to do a job which would require more skill and coolness, more hard work and danger, than was demanded of any other voluntary organisation. In the event of "Action Stations" being ordered you knew well the kind of life you were in for. But that was in order; you were picked men and others, including myself, knew that you would continue to fight whatever the conditions, with, or if necessary without, orders. It now falls to me to tell you that your work has been appreciated and well carried out and that your contract, for the moment, is at an end. I am grateful to you for the way you have trained in the last four years. So is the Regular Army. It was due to you that more divisions left this country to fight the battle of France; and it was due to your reputation for skill and determination that extra risk was taken – sucessfully as it turned out – in the defence arrangements of this country during that vital period. I congratulate you on this reputation and thank you for this voluntary effort. In view of the fact that your lives depended on secrecy, no public recognition will be possible. But those in the responsible positions at General Headquarters, Home Forces, know what was done and what would have been done had you been called upon. . . . It will not be forgotten.'

Indeed, those who served in the Auxiliary Units were not forgotten; it was simply that their existence was unknown to the public at large. Bound by the Official Secrets Act, former members held their silence long after the war had ended, and many years were to elapse before information about this underground British Resistance entered the public domain. Old habits die hard and, although now released from the embargo placed upon them by the country's wartime security regulations, even today many of those surviving members who served in the 'Secret Army' speak with obvious reluctance about their experiences with this élite guerrilla force.

CHAPTER 10

Last Orders

The assumption must surely have been, by most of those who were serving in the Home Guard, that the force would remain intact until the war drew to an end. On 14 May 1943, in a speech delivered from Washington to mark the Home Guard's third anniversary and to boost morale among the men, Prime Minister Churchill (who was staying at the White House with the United States' President) spoke in glowing terms about Britain's civilian army. (From its inception Churchill was always one of the force's staunchest allies). 'The degree of the invasion danger depends entirely upon the strength or weakness of the forces and preparations gathered to meet it. . . . You Home Guardsmen are a vital part of those forces; you are specially adapted to meet that most modern form of overseas attack – the mass descent of parachute troops.'

In what proved to be a long speech, Churchill went on to explain that the very existence of the Home Guard released large numbers of men from the Regular Forces to be deployed '. . . for the assault on the strongholds of the enemy's power. It is this reason which, above all others, has prompted me to make you and all Britain realise afresh, by this Home Guard celebration . . . the part you have to play in the supreme cause now gathering momentum. . . .'

In a statement issued on 14 May 1944, the force's Colonel-in-Chief, King George VI, had explained that '. . . the fourth anniversary of the Home Guard falls in a year when the duties assigned to you have a very real importance. . . .' He went on to express his confidence that everyone involved would '. . . carry on in the same high spirit of patriotism that you have always shown, until the day of victory.'

However, as the second half of 1944 wore on, the outlook for the Home Guard seemed increasingly uncertain. In a Special Order of the Day issued on 14 August, Lieutenant-General Sir E.C.A. Schreiber, Commander-in-Chief of units throughout south-east England, wrote to his men: 'For the future, while it is impossible that [Germany] can attempt full-scale invasion, the possibility of sabotage or raids, which can be regarded as a local invasion, must remain, especially in south-east England. It is for this reason that the Home Guard is still required.

'The time will come, however, when the Home Guard will no longer be needed to defend our country from an invader. This may coincide with the end of the war in Europe, or it may be earlier. The decision must rest with the War Cabinet. But the time for this has not yet come. While there remains even the smallest danger of a Hun [sic] attempting to set his foot in the country, the Home Guard will continue to be necessary. . . . I promise that there will be no delay in letting the Home Guard know when they are no longer required; but until then – Carry on!'

As it turned out, however, events were to move swiftly. Just over three weeks later, on 6 September, the Secretary of State for War, Sir James Grigg, announced over the wireless that '. . . the end, so far as Germany is concerned, cannot be far off but it may be that before the end arrives even voluntary duty in the Home Guard can be discontinued. Operations on the Continent have developed in a very spectacular manner, and have brought the Allies to the very gates of Germany. This means that the Government is in a position to review its arrangements for warding off hostile attack. The Home Guard has formed a large part of these arrangements. . . . The Government has always assured the Home Guard that as soon as their services are no longer required they will be told. The time has not yet arrived . . . but there is no longer any need to call on them for compulsory drills and training. . . . The Home Guard will not be asked to do a day's more work than is necessary, and they may be sure that they will be told the moment the time has come.'

In fact, that time was not long in arriving and, towards the end of October, it was officially announced that the Home Guard would be stood down the following month. In a Special Home Guard Order of the Day dated 23 November, Lieutenant-General W.D. Morgan, Commander-in-Chief of Southern Command, wrote: 'Since 1940 the Home Guard of Southern Command has had its own special responsibilities. For three years you were ready to take the first impact of invasion, and your preparedness played its part in preventing the enemy from making the attempt. . . . The work was often dull and monotonous. It was none the less important. Not only did you safeguard the preparations for the Second Front but also, by releasing Field Armies from this work, you allowed them to return to the Continent in the fullest possible strength. . . .'

General Sir Harold Franklyn, Commander-in-Chief of Home Forces, expanded the theme. 'During the past few years I have had many opportunities of seeing the Home Guard in most parts of the country, including Northern Ireland. . . . A high standard of efficiency has been reached, which has been made possible only by the keenness and devotion to duty of all ranks. . . . The Home Guard came into being at a time of acute crisis in our history, and for over four years has stood prepared to repel any invader to our shores. The reliance that has been placed on you during these years has been abundantly justified. . . . Now you can stand down with every right to feel that you have done your duty and contributed materially to history.'

The King, in his capacity as the Home Guard's Colonel-in-Chief, added his own tribute in a Special Army Order of the Day dated 14 November. 'For more than four years you have borne a heavy burden. Most of you have been engaged for long hours in work necessary to the prosecution of war, or to maintaining the healthful life of the Nation; and you have given a great portion of the time which should have been your own to learning the skilled work of a soldier. By this patient, ungrudging effort you have built and maintained a force able to play an essential part in the defence of our threatened soil and liberty. Now, at last . . .

Special Order of the Day to 19th (WW) Battalion Hampshire Home Guard

by

Lt.-Colonel F. Nevill Jennings, M.C. (Commanding)

P.B. Drill Hall,
Newport, I.W.
31st December, 1944.

During the 4½ years it has been my privilege to command the Battalion—I have had ample opportunity to appreciate the keenness and devotion to duty displayed by all ranks, a keenness which, considering the restricted time available for training, has resulted in a very high standard of efficiency.

We can look back with satisfaction to having made a contribution towards winning the war which is recognised by all.

I am very proud to have commanded the Battalion during the critical times from which the country has emerged.

On the occasion of the "Standing Down", I want to thank all ranks for their keenness and co-operation—and to wish every one of you the best of luck in the future.

F. Nevill Jennings

Lt.-Col.

Special Orders of the Day were issued by Commanding Officers of all Home Guard battalions at Stand Down, thanking the men for their tireless efforts during the four-and-a-half years of the force's existence.

I can say that you have fulfilled your charge. The Home Guard has reached the end of its long tour of duty under arms. But I know that your devotion to our land, your comradeship, your power to work your hardest at the end of the longest day, will discover new outlets for patriotic service in time of peace. History will say that your share in the greatest of all our struggles for freedom was a vitally important one. . . .'

The news of the Home Guard's imminent demise was received with a mixture of emotions by the men themselves. Few could doubt that, by this stage of the war, the Home Guard had drawn to the end of its useful life and that, from an economic standpoint, no real case could be made to maintain the force any longer. Some felt that their services were being dispensed with prematurely, given that the war was still in progress. However, for the most part discontent was tempered with relief, particularly by those men who were holding down full-time jobs (i.e. the majority of the force) in addition to serving with the Home Guard.

Nevertheless, the decision to stand down the Home Guard came as an unwelcome surprise for some of its members. Derek Osborne, who served with a platoon near High Wycombe, explains: 'Attending for duty one evening, we were called outside for an informal parade. Reading from a paper that he held, our Company Commander told us that the Home Guard was to be stood down with almost immediate effect. Arrangements would be made for us to hand in our uniforms and equipment at a later date. His statement was delivered coldly and clearly and was received by everyone present in total silence. I don't think that even the officers had any prior knowledge of this decision from out of the blue. It is strange that nobody had given a thought to the probability of this event. After all, we were winning the war and the conflict would not go on for ever. Neither would the need for our services, of course, yet we had not foreseen this sudden almost brutal announcement. In civilian terms, it was similar to a manager walking up to an employee and saying "You're fired!"'

Major C.L. Hawkins of the 13th North Staffordshire (Cannock) Battalion Home Guard confirms that '. . . the Stand Down order came as a surprise to most members . . . and the manner of its coming was not popular with all ranks. However, once the inevitability of a Stand Down was accepted, farewell parties became the order of the day. . . . One knew after attending them that if Stand Down were cancelled as a result of a change in the military situation, every man would be back with a smile.'

Despite the privations of wartime, dinners were conjured up and eaten, toasts were drunk and valedictory speeches made by the score. Wherever these celebrations were held, the atmosphere would have been much the same as that reported in the *Hampshire Herald*, following the Colemore Platoon's Stand Down supper and social held at East Tisted Village Hall. After the toasts had been proposed, and each member of the platoon had been mentioned individually by name, Lieutenant C.R. Woodcock, who presided over the evening, concluded his address by saying that '. . . These are the men with whom it has been my privilege to serve, my honour to command, and as this is perhaps the last time on which we shall all be together, you can imagine that I feel this occasion deeply. It is because I know so well the spirit that has gone to make this platoon that I feel able to give a pledge, namely, that should ever these islands be threatened again – it matters not from what point of the compass that threat may come – those who have served in Colemore Platoon will be among the very first to take up such arms as may be available in the defence of this old England of ours.' This was stirring stuff indeed, and one can be quite certain that the same sentiments were being expressed in similar words at farewell suppers from Penzance to the Outer Hebrides and Northern Isles.

Arrangements were hastily made for Stand Down parades to be held in towns and cities throughout the country. Events of one kind or another spanned several months and lasted until the end of the year, but Sunday 3 December was officially set aside for the ceremonial parades marking Stand Down. Inevitably, the focus of national attention was centred on London, where the King and Queen and

Members of the Inveraray Home Guard, Argyll, assemble for their final parade at Stand Down.

the two Princesses attended the parade which made its way to Hyde Park after seven thousand members of the Home Guard, drawn from units throughout the United Kingdom, had marched in columns through the West End. Men of all ranks from as far apart as Shetland and Cornwall were invited to attend the event, and a small but representative number of these were further selected to be present at the Lord Mayor's banquet which was held on the eve of the great day. Captain W.A. Owen was one of these privileged guests, and his account of that memorable weekend, published in the Choughs Annual Register at the end of 1944 – 'Choughs', incidentally, was the name by which the 11th Cornwall (Newquay) Battalion Home Guard was known, in homage to Cornwall's native bird – gives a vivid eye-witness acount of the proceedings. 'I must admit that when I was detailed by the CO to represent Cornwall in the Stand Down parade in London I felt a bit nervous. I had no particular qualms about the military side, but the thought of a Lord Mayor's banquet etc. did rather shake me. However, I determined to do my utmost to justify the CO's confidence, and the great honour that was mine in leading forty-two other Cornish boys past the King.

'I travelled up through the Friday night and, after a spell of sight-seeing, reported at the Annexe to the Brigade of Guards' Mess in Sloane Street during the Saturday afternoon. . . . After tea I prepared for the great event of the evening, and at seven o'clock precisely arrived at the Mansion House to dine with the Lord Mayor. . . . The dinner was first-class: turtle soup accompanied by sherry, roast turkey and vegetables with red or white wine, a delicious sweet that I could not possibly identify, followed by coffee and cigars. . . .

'Sunday, the great day, did not look too promising at day-break. . . . I walked across to Chelsea Barracks and found the Cornish contingent in great spirits. They had been royally treated, with as much food as they wanted and even a cup of tea in bed. . . .

'After lunch [we all] moved off for the Parade Ground. This entailed a march of three miles which, in view of our heavy greatcoats and steel helmets, proved a bit of a trial. The saluting base was at Stanhope Gate, just in front of the statue

7,000 representatives drawn from Home Guard battalions nationwide took part in the great Stand Down parade held in London on Sunday 3 December 1944. Here, columns of Home Guard are seen marching past the saluting base at Stanhope Gate.

of St George and the Dragon which, together with the presence of the King and Queen and the two Princesses, made a most symbolic picture. . . . Bursting with pride, we swung past His Majesty in what was probably the most intense moment of my Home Guard career. Swinging on to Piccadilly, we heard the cheers and applause of the crowd, ten to fifteen deep all the way. Soon we were marching at ease, and all through Regent Street and Oxford Street and back to Hyde Park the crowds were as thick as ever, and did they cheer us! Finally we reached the Serpentine, where a Home Guard band was playing "Auld Lang Syne", and from there had another one and a half miles to walk back to barracks. By this time I must admit we were feeling the strain and I, at least, had collected a couple of blisters. We had been on parade for five hours and marched nine miles. . . .'

Even then the day had not quite finished. In the evening the men attended a show at the Albert Hall, where the comedians Robb Wilton and Tommy Trinder and musical-comedy actress Cicely Courtneidge were among the stars who turned out for this special occasion.

The King's farewell message to the Home Guard was broadcast over the wireless at nine o'clock, and relayed to the audience gathered inside the Albert Hall. 'Over four years ago . . . a call went out for men to enrol themselves in a new citizen army . . . to stand against the invader in every village and every town. . . . Almost overnight a new force came into being, a force which had little equipment but was mighty in courage and determination. . . . For most of you

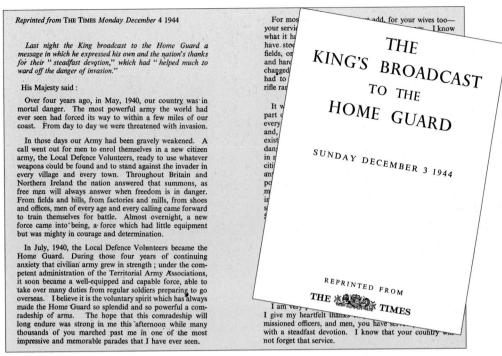

The Times *transcript of the King's farewell broadcast to the Home Guard.*

your service in the Home Guard has not been easy. . . . Some of you have stood for many hours on the gun sites, in desolate fields, or windswept beaches. Many of you, after a long and hard day's work, scarcely had time for food before you changed into uniform for the evening parade. . . .'

In effect, the King's farewell message marked the closing of an era. In the months immediately prior to the Stand Down, the Home Guard's strength exceeded one and a half million men (not to mention the many Women Auxiliaries who were officially installed by that time). Measured by any standards, this was a massive civilian army committed to defending the Home Front. Now nothing remained to be done except to make arrangements for reunion dinners and set up Old Comrades' associations, and wait for the personal message of thanks, issued on behalf of the King in recognition of services rendered, to drop through the letter-box.

'When history comes to be written,' reflected A.G. Street, 'what will it say, what can it say, of a military force that existed under arms for nearly five years during the greatest war the world has known, and yet from its inception to its disbanding was never tried in battle [with the notable exception, of course, of those many Home Guard members who manned anti-aircraft batteries]. I hope the verdict will be that by its existence it had a major effect on the course of that war during its most dangerous years; for that is what most Home Guards believe to be true. . . .'

DINNER

given by

Messrs. & SAMUEL WHITE Co. Ltd.

to mark the occasion of the

STAND DOWN

of

The West Cowes (J. S. White) V.P. Coy.,
XIX Bn. Hampshire Home Guard.

SHIPYARD CANTEEN.
16th February, 1945.

Programme cover for the Stand Down dinner held at Messrs Samuel White & Co. Ltd, on the Isle of Wight. This company's Home Guard unit formed part of the 19th Battalion Hampshire Home Guard.

In the years when our Country

was in mortal danger

Percy Robert Benjamin Iddon

who served 30.5.40 --- 31.12.44.

gave generously of his time and

powers to make himself ready

for her defence by force of arms

and with his life if need be.

George R.I.

THE HOME GUARD

Every Home Guard received a copy of this certificate from the King at Stand Down. Percy Iddon, the recipient on this occasion, served from the very early days of the LDV until the force was disbanded.

Writing in 1943, at a time when the force was still actively in existence, Captain Simon Fine was in no doubt of its value and unique attributes. 'No spontaneous call to arms in defence of a motherland has ever equalled the mighty birth, and mightier growth, of the Home Guard of Britain. Its strength is the strength of the people, its discipline the symbol of the nation. It is more than an army for defence. It is an idea that must never be allowed to perish.'

Albert Squires, who was a young Home Guard at Ibstock in Leicestershire, is in no doubt that, had they been put to the test, the members of his platoon would have acquitted themselves admirably. 'The majority of our unit were First World War veterans, and their patriotism had to be seen to be believed. . . . I really believe that if we had been invaded those men would have given a good account of themselves even with the limited and out of date weaponry that they had. . . . As a nation we should be proud of them.'

The historian of the 6th Battalion Monmouthshire Home Guard struck an elegiac note. 'The final answer as to whether the Home Guard was worthwhile rests with us, and us alone. If only the spirit and feeling engendered during these past years of war and service could be carried at this time into our private lives, if we meet one another in the future as we did during those days, if our greetings are as sincere, if our capacity for understanding and sacrifice are brought to bear on the problems that will undoubtedly confront the nation during the coming years, if the two million who served are determined that the friendliness, comradeship and kindly feeling that existed shall not be lost . . . then, indeed, the Home Guard would finally and for all time have justified its existence and would, in truth, have been worthwhile.'

*   *   *

The celebrated and oft-repeated TV series *Dad's Army* provokes a wide range of opinions among surviving former members of the Home Guard. Many catch odd glimpses of themselves, or of people they served with, in this comic compendium of fondly drawn characters, and they cherish the gentle and affectionate humour with which Britain's wartime civilian army is portrayed. Because it all happened so long ago, it is only the younger members of the Home Guard who are still alive today, and I have lost count of the number of times that men have said to me – when identifying themselves in their Home Guard photographs – that 'I am the Pike character in the back row', or 'I am the "stupid boy" at the front'. Cedric Comley, a Home Guard in Bristol, recalled a Lance Corporal Jones-type character in his platoon who was an inveterate interrupter of the 'permission to speak' variety. '. . . We also had a private who very much resembled Mr Godfrey. He was a gentleman who had been an officer in the Boer War forty years earlier. Like Godfrey he was seldom off parade, did his share of night duty and tried manfully to do the more strenuous exercises. He might have been better employed relaxing in his chair at home, for after some months with us he died peacefully.'

William Martin of East Lothian remembers a Private Walker character in his platoon, '. . . a "wide boy" who was always prepared to take a chance.' Having promised to obtain a Christmas goose for a fellow platoon member (a coal-merchant by trade) at the princely cost of £5, 'Walker' turned up on his comrade's doorstep late on Christmas Eve '. . . holding a dead bird by its neck. Only later, when the coal-merchant inspected the "goose" in his kitchen did he realise it was a swan, presumably captured from the pond in the local park. So ended his Christmas treat.'

Meanwhile, there are some former Home Guards who feel that *Dad's Army* has perhaps strayed a little too far from the truth in its pursuit of comedy, and are unhappy about the image of incompetence that they feel it perpetuates. Thus, Bert Donkin of Chelmsford: 'With the exception of the Civil Defence Warden, Mr Hodges, not one person – the blustering, self-important captain organising one disaster after another; the effete, laid-back sergeant in a permanent state of lethargy; the gibbering, hysterical lance-corporal – bears the slightest resemblance to anyone I met in the Home Guard.'

The Revd Fred Beddow believes that '. . . *Dad's Army* is a caricature and, as such, contains some truth, but it does the reality a disservice because it cannot reproduce the spirit which motivated us. I never met a Captain Mainwaring and, for all that we were as diverse a bunch as you could ever hope to meet in age, background and education, none were as incompetent as some of the men portrayed in the TV series. . . . By the time I left the Home Guard in 1942, it had become in reality a force which would have given a good account of itself to any invading army.'

However, surely even the programme's most trenchant dissenters would concede that in the last episode of the final series the writers paid a moving tribute to the Home Guard, and reminded their mass audience decades after the force had been disbanded just what the real Dad's Army had stood for in Britain's greatest hour of need. Members of the Walmington-on-Sea platoon were gathered together after watching over the coast during an invasion alert. Along came Warden Hodges to tell Mainwaring's men that it had all been a false alarm, adding characteristically as he departed that it was lucky for them because, if the Nazis ever did arrive, they would 'walk straight through' the Walmington-on-Sea platoon. The men were furious, but Mainwaring dismissed the Warden's remarks with contempt. 'Anyone who tries to take our homes or our freedom away from us will find out what we can do,' he told the platoon. 'There are men all over Britain, men who will stand together when their country needs them.' That, in a nutshell, was the essence of the Home Guard; a force which we have come to look back on as something of an historical or military aberration, but one which nevertheless drew from its members a deep store of altruism. Bert Donkin again: 'The Home Guard must have been one of the few institutions that promised no pay, no pensions, no benefits and no rewards. A minimal amount of prestige went with promotion, I suppose, but no one clamoured for it, in fact many actively avoided it. All ranks were in the same boat, which was not a particularly watertight vessel.'

CHAPTER 11

Time, Gentlemen, Please – A Postscript

Contrary to popular belief the Stand Down, which took effect during the closing months of 1944, was not quite the end of the Home Guard's story. In 1952, when fears were mounting that Britain could possibly be on the receiving end of a Russian invasion, the Home Guard was resurrected. The new force was structured differently from its wartime predecessor, and it failed not only to attract as much support as the Government had hoped, but also never achieved anything like the same high profile in the public consciousness.

W.J. Amesbury served with the 12/13 Somerset Home Guard Cadre Battalion in the postwar version of the force. 'The role of the Home Guard in the 1950s differed from that of the 1940s inasmuch that during the war members of the force were seen on duty by the public at sensitive and strategic locations. However, in the 1950s we were only seen when out on exercises or attending the annual Remembrance services. Nevertheless, we were always training and attending lectures, in order to keep abreast of the current political situation.'

Richard Nicholson, who was a member of the 12th West Riding Battalion Home Guard, confesses that '. . . we never really knew what our role was, but we assumed that if we were ever invaded by the Russian hordes . . . we would make them pay dearly for entering Wharfedale.'

Meanwhile, in Sussex, local schoolmaster Roger Ray was a member of the Handcross Home Guard based at Ashfold House, a boys' preparatory school lying between Horsham and Haywards Heath. Mr Ray recalls his time spent in Britain's postwar Home Guard with much obvious affection. 'Ashfold House was once the home of Lord Nelson's sister and was often visited by the famous man in between his "sorties". What he would have said if he had come back on one of those summer evenings in 1952 and seen this "de-luxe" Home Guard training on the immaculate lawns, and in the squash court, would have been interesting to hear.

'This ten-strong outpost, stationed a mile or so south of Handcross, had a mammoth task . . . to defend Warninglid Ridge in time of invasion! They were to be backed up by companies from Crawley and Rowfant.

'To carry out their duties of helping to defend airfields, combatting airborne and seaborne raids, protecting vulnerable points against sabotage and rendering help to Civil Defence, the ten men were kept on their toes. In charge of this army,

Schoolmasters Lewis Creed and Roger Ray 'defending' Warninglid Ridge in Sussex, 1952.

A briefing session for members of the Handcross Home Guard at Ashfold House, 1950s.

Pass the salt! With their duty done for the day, these four members of the 'ten-man army' at Ashfold House enjoy a convivial meal together, 1950s.

half of them ex-wartime men, was Captain Richard Sykes, joint headmaster of the school. Promotion was fairly rapid and I think there was only one private when we disbanded in 1956.

'This was no ordinary Home Guard; with training over for the night, the men would repair to the Master's club where a pint of ale and a three-course meal were waiting and, after talking about future campaigns and cricket, we – who didn't live at the school – would creep home to our "Home Guard widows".

'Yes, I was one of that ten-man army, and I have a certificate from the Secretary of State for War to prove it, thanking me for the willing service I gave to my country. Sadly, Ashfold is no longer there. It was taken down brick by brick a few years later. If only they had said, we could have saved them a lot of trouble – it would have made a super exercise.'

Women were also recruited to the 1950s' version of the Home Guard, and served a similar function to that which they had performed during the war. Peggy McGeoch (formerly Wightman), who now lives in South Africa, recalls her Home Guard days in Norwich, where she was trained to do office work and also to operate two-way radios. '. . . We were taught to take them apart, and I could easily repair the more run-of-the-mill failures. I seem to remember that I could strip down the radio into its component parts in thirty-five minutes, but I don't remember putting it together again! . . . I can also recall the serious, dedicated atmosphere at the lectures which I attended, and the comradeship was wonderful.'

2nd Lieut Margaret Wightman on Home Guard duty in Norwich with Major Scott (centre) and Lieut Col Coe (left), 1950s.

2nd Lieut Margaret Wightman and Sgt Green operating two-way radios while on Home Guard duty in Norwich, 1950s.

Unlike the wartime Home Guard, which had been raised in response to a specific and dauntingly imminent threat to Britain's national security and future independence, (and for which reasons the call to form a civilian army had undoubtedly caught the mood of the moment), the 1950s' force was designed to help combat a danger that was – if no less real – somehow vaguer and more at arm's length. In 1952, after all, there were no masses of enemy troops gathered just a few hours away on the other side of the English Channel. As a result, and despite the best efforts of all concerned, the post-war force came and went without too much fuss.

* * *

There can be no doubt that the Home Guard casts a very long shadow, and one that has been indisputably lengthened by the ever-popular *Dad's Army*. Whether a civilian force of this kind would ever have a part to play in a modern or any future conflict is open to question, and so it is likely that this honourable tradition which reaches back to those Somerset men who were raised against Monmouth and the trained bands of Elizabeth I (and possibly beyond), has come to the end of its distinguished line. However, there was a moment during the spring of 1982 when the spirit of the Home Guard was awakened – albeit briefly and perhaps lightheartedly – in at least one small corner of England. Argentina had invaded the Falkland Islands and, in the early weeks of April, the Royal Navy Task Force set off on its long haul down to the South Atlantic. Meanwhile, the denizens of my local pub – the King Harold's Head – at Nazeing in Essex, many of them anxious to 'do their bit', decided to form a Home Guard platoon, the details of which were duly posted on a wall in the bar. But, as most people in the village agreed, the 'volunteers' had probably been looking through the bottom of too many empty glasses at the time, or watching a surfeit of *Dad's Army* on television. Needless to say, the platoon evaporated almost before the first parade had been called!

If nothing else, however, this incident only goes to show that the irrepressible spirit referred to by the King during his Stand Down broadcast in December 1944 – that free men will always answer the summons when freedom is in danger – was lurking only just below the surface, even in that materially self-centred and self-obsessed decade of the 1980s. So, watch this space . . .

Lieut. W.J. Amesbury.

I wish to express my sincere appreciation of the loyal and willing service which you gave to the Country as an active member of the Home Guard, during the period 1952 – 1956.

Antony Head

The War Office,   Secretary of State
London.   for War.

Lieut W.J. Amesbury of the 12/13 Somerset Home Guard Cadre Battalion, together with everyone else who served in the postwar version of 'Dad's Army', received a copy of this letter of thanks from War Minister Antony Head.

Bibliography

Angell, Stewart, *The Secret Sussex Resistance 1940–1944*, Middleton Press, Midhurst, 1996.

Beardmore, George, *Civilians at War: Journals 1938–1946*, John Murray, 1984.

Bishop, N.R., *A Short History of the 8th Surrey* (Reigate) Battalion Home Guard, 1944.

Choughs (11th Cornwall Battalion Home Guard) Annual Register Volume 2, 1944.

Fine, Capt Simon, *With the Home Guard*, Alliance Press Ltd., 1943.

Graves, Charles, *The Home Guard of Britain*, Hutchinson, 1943.

History of the 13th North Staffordshire (Cannock) Battalion Home Guard, 1945.

Jenkins, Capt Warren, *The 6th Battalion Monmouthshire Home Guard 1940–1944*, N/D.

Lampe, David, *The Last Ditch*, Cassell, 1968.

Longmate, Norman, *The Real Dad's Army*, Arrow Books, 1974.

Mackay, Major E.A., *The History of the Wiltshire Home Guard*, Wiltshire County Territorial Association, 1946.

Mackay, Major G.S., *General Knowledge for Home Guards*, N/D.

Mackenzie, S.P., *The Home Guard*, Oxford University Press, 1996.

Minns, Raynes, *Bombers & Mash: The Domestic Front 1939–1945*, Virago Press, 1980.

Orwell, Sonia & Angus, Ian, (eds), *The Collected Essays, Journalism and Letters of George Orwell Volume 2: My Country Right or Left 1940–1943*, Secker & Warburg, 1968.

Raymond, Ernest, *Please You Draw Near*, Cassell 1969.

Searle, Adrian, *The Island at War*, Dovecote Press, Ltd., Wimborne, 1989.

Shaw, Frank & Joan, *We Remember the Home Guard*, Isis Large print Edn., 1991.

Story of the First Berkshire (Abingdon) Battalion Home Guard, 1945.

Street, A.G., *From Dusk Till Dawn*, Blandford Press, 1945.

Turner, E.S., *The Phoney War*, Michael Joseph, 1961.

Uttley, Alison, *Hare Joins the Home Guard*, Collins, 1941.

Index

Index of Place Names